32-52

A CHRISTIAN VIEW OF HISTORY?

EDITORS

George Marsden
Frank Roberts

WILLIAM B. EERDMANS PUBLISHING COMPANY
Grand Rapids, Michigan

Dedicated to Henry Ippel

Library of Congress Cataloging in Publication Data
Main entry under title:
A Christian view of history?

    Includes index.
    1. History (Theology) — Addresses, essays, lectures.
2. History (Theology) — History of doctrines — 20th century —
Addresses, essays, lectures. I. Marsden,
George M., 1939-   II. Roberts, Frank C.,
1937-
BR115.H5C55   231'.7   75-19419
ISBN 0-8028-1603-7

The essay by Dirk W. Jellema was published previously under the
title, "The Christian and History," *The Reformed Journal*, December,
1971. The essay by George M. Marsden was published in the *Christian
Scholar's Review*, Vol. II, No. 4, 1973, under the title, "The Christian
and the Teaching of History." C. T. McIntire's essay is also available
from the Wedge Publishing Foundation, Toronto, Ontario, Canada.
The essay by William A. Speck on Kenneth Scott Latourette, and the
essay by Dale K. Van Kley, are also being published by the *Christian
Scholar's Review*.

Contents

The Authors

FRANK C. ROBERTS: *Associate Professor of History at Calvin College. Ph.D., Vanderbilt University.*

DIRK W. JELLEMA: *Professor of History at Calvin College. Ph.D., University of Wisconsin.*

GEORGE M. MARSDEN: *Professor of History at Calvin College. Ph.D., Yale University.*

C. T. MCINTIRE: *Senior Member in History and Historiography at the Institute for Christian Studies, Toronto. Ph.D., University of Pennsylvania.*

DONALD A. MACPHEE: *Dean of the School of Social and Behavioral Sciences, California State College, Dominguiz Hills. Ph.D., University of California at Berkeley.*

EDWIN J. VAN KLEY: *Professor of History at Calvin College. Ph.D., University of Chicago.*

WILLIAM A. SPECK: *Professor of History at the University of South Alabama. Ph.D., Florida State University.*

DALE K. VAN KLEY: *Associate Professor of History at Calvin College. Ph.D., Yale University.*

M. HOWARD RIENSTRA: *Professor of History at Calvin College. Ph.D., University of Michigan.*

Introduction

FRANK C. ROBERTS

I

CHRISTIAN SCHOLARS in every age have been intensely concerned with the questions, How does my Christianity bear on my scholarship? and Is it possible for me to integrate faith and learning? Their answers have differed widely. This volume of essays, which is the fruit of much reflection and many years of dialogue among Christian historians, is presented as a contemporary attempt to suggest meaningful and helpful answers to the above questions as they relate to the study and teaching of history.[1] The authors of these essays have in common a belief that Christianity must relate to the Christian historian's functions as a scholar and a teacher. They also share a conviction that it is not only a possibility, but an absolute necessity to integrate one's faith with one's scholarly endeavors.

It is the hope of the editors that this collection of essays will prove useful to Christian historians as well as to other students of history as they seek more fully to understand the relationship between Christianity and history. The book is not presented, however, as a collection of definitive answers concerning a Christian approach to history. The authors of the essays contained in this volume frankly acknowledge the tentative character of much of what they have written. In contrast to definitiveness, this volume is presented for the purpose of stimulating and broadening discussion of the relationship between Christianity and history.

It is important to point out that the essays in this volume are written from the perspective of orthodox Protestantism,

1. Several of the essays in this volume were written by professors of history at Calvin College. These essays are the fruit of an ongoing dialogue within the Calvin College History Department on the subject of a Christian approach to the study of history. It was within the context of these discussions that the idea for this book took form.

or from what some would perhaps prefer to call an evangelical perspective. The authors have in common a belief in the authority of Scripture and a conviction that biblical revelation must be the starting point for the Christian historian. It is appropriate that a book on Christianity and history written from this perspective should appear at a time when the evangelical community is becoming increasingly interested in issues and concerns that in the past it too frequently chose to ignore. Many within this community are no longer satisfied with a dualistic world-view that tends to isolate a "spiritual" or "religious" realm from the so-called neutral areas of life. Instead, one sees within this tradition a growing desire to relate Christianity to all areas of life, including the domain of scholarship. The success of the Conference on Faith and History, as well as its journal, *Fides et Historia,* gives ample evidence that this same concern is present in the community of Christian historians. It is hoped that this book will contribute to the achievement of the goals set forth by that organization, as well as enhance the spirit of seeking evident among Christian scholars today.

II

Christian historians who have been concerned with the subject of Christianity and history have frequently erred either in the direction of overassurance or in the direction of over-diffidence.[2] The tendency toward overassurance has generally been marked both by its disposition to play down the complexity and ambiguity of history and by its inclination to emphasize the clarity of the divine plan and purpose in events of the past. Historians who have inclined toward overassurance have viewed a Christian approach to history as essentially the unveiling of the divine plan within specific events of the past, and the pointing out of the good and evil forces within history.

The tendency toward overassurance has frequently been found among Christian historians within the evangelical tra-

2. These two tendencies are discussed by E. Harris Harbison in *Christianity and History* (Princeton, 1964), p. 14.

dition. Its most blatant and popular form is that interpretation of history called "dispensationalism." For, although Hal Lindsey, the most popular and well-known advocate of this approach to history, is not in any technical sense an historian, his work is as clear a manifestation of a self-assured approach to history as one could find. Claiming that the dispensational viewpoint is solidly based on a high view of Scripture, he not only unravels in minute detail the meaning and purpose of past events, but he also claims, without a hint of trepidation or doubt, the ability to ascertain the meaning of current events (especially in the Near East), while elaborating in great detail on the occurrences that await the world both in the immediate and more distant future.[3]

More modest and academically respectable examples of the tendency toward overassurance may also be found within the evangelical tradition. To some degree, Kenneth Scott Latourette, the great church historian and East Asian scholar, can be seen as representing this viewpoint. With a degree of self-confidence that would perhaps astound many Christian historians, Latourette distinguishes in his writings between the forces of good and the forces of evil, while also claiming the ability to trace with some degree of accuracy the results within history of the transforming power of Christ. He also claims the ability as a Christian historian to see the hand of God at work in history, leading the forces of good to ever greater power and strength throughout the earth.[4]

3. The phenomenal sale of Hal Lindsey's book *The Late Great Planet Earth* (Grand Rapids, 1971) gives ample evidence of the popularity of this approach to history within the evangelical community. It is the opinion of the editors that, despite the popularity of dispensationalism, it is not really successful as an effort to relate Christianity and history in a scholarly way. It is probably fair to suggest that dispensationalism largely ignores the accepted canons of historical scholarship in its rather facile attempts to relate the Bible to current and future events.
4. See the presidential address delivered by Latourette before the American Historical Association in 1948, in *American Historical Review*, January, 1949, pp. 259-276, for the basic outlines of his approach to history. See also the essay in this volume by William Speck, "Kenneth Scott Latourette's Vocation as a Christian Historian." Whatever one may think of Latourette's inclination to be somewhat overassured in relating Christianity and history, his significance as an historian cannot be questioned.

The Dooyeweerdian[5] school of historical interpretation has at times also demonstrated this tendency toward overassurance. It seems clear that this approach to the past has been both somewhat reductionistic and presumptuous. One finds in this movement, for example, the belief that certain mysterious forces that lie behind the actions of man in history have been located. At least one Dooyeweerdian historian, for example, claims that Dooyeweerd has made the "discovery and formulation of the religious ground-motives that have driven and determined all of Western Civilization."[6] The task of the Christian historian is to trace these forces as they unfold in history. In addition, some in this school suppose that they have knowledge of the "norms" (God's will and law) that determine how historical development must take place.[7] With this basic apparatus (ground-motives and norms) the Dooyeweerdian historian moves through the past judging this society as flawed, that form of Christianity as "synthetic," this political development as progressive or regressive, and so forth. Given these basic interpretative tools, there remains very little ambiguity in history.

As noted earlier, overassurance is not the only error into which Christian historians may fall. There is also the tendency among certain Christian historians toward overdiffidence with respect to the relationship between Christianity and history. If the overly assured are frequently extremely confident of their ability to approach and interpret history from a Christian perspective, the overly diffident Christian historians are inclined to reject a Christian approach to history as impossible, absurd, and probably undesirable.

The historian Karl Löwith represents one example of such an approach to Christianity and history. In his opinion, a Christian approach to history must be rejected as "nonsense" since the New Testament itself declares such an endeavor

5. Although the work of Herman Dooyeweerd, a Dutch philosopher, is not widely known outside the Reformed community, he has developed by far the most comprehensive system relating Christianity to all areas of learning to appear in the twentieth century. See the essay in this volume by Dale Van Kley, "Dooyeweerd as Historian."
6. John Van Dyk, *A Christian Approach to Medieval History* (Sioux Center, Ia., 1971), p. 9.
7. Van Dyk, pp. 12ff.

to be an impossibility. The New Testament, says Löwith, views events in the world as chaotic, ruled by Satan, and therefore resistant to a Christian approach. In fact, history is the recording of events that are essentially the antithesis of Christianity. Can history and Christianity be related? Löwith must say "never," because the attempt to relate them violates the givens of the Christian faith.[8]

Van Harvey suggests another reason why some Christian historians are disinclined to relate their faith to their scholarship in a conscious way. Many Christian historians simply feel that there is an incompatibility between the "new morality of critical judgement which has seized the imagination of the scholar in the Western world," and "the ethic of belief that has dominated Christendom for centuries."[9] Many historians have felt the need to separate their Christian belief from their scholarship, since they have come to accept the argument that belief, when consciously related to scholarship, inevitably "corrodes the delicate machinery of sound historical judgement."[10]

III

The authors of the essays in this volume are committed to a mediating position vis-à-vis a Christian approach to history. They seek to avoid the extremes of overassurance and over-diffidence. While retaining an awareness of the complexity and ambiguity of history, they are unwilling to view human activity as chaotic and under the control of demonic powers. Nor are they willing to accept as valid the observation that Christian commitment must undermine sound scholarship. At the same time, however, they are hesitant to claim that

8. See Karl Löwith, *Meaning in History* (Chicago, 1957), pp. 191-203. Löwith does suggest that in a sense the rejection of history is a Christian approach to history.

9. Van A. Harvey, *The Historian and the Believer* (New York, 1969), p. 38.

10. Harvey, p. 119. By the nature of the case, historians who accept the viewpoint of Löwith, or that described by Harvey, are not likely to produce much scholarship explicitly relating their Christianity to their historical scholarship. This silence should not suggest to anyone, however, that this school of thought has few adherents. It is to these thinkers that the first part of this book is directed.

the hand of God or the forces of good and evil are easily
identified within history. In their opinion, no church, state,
person, or viewpoint can be identified as the repository of good
or evil, or as the agent in some unique way of the divine.
Rather, they are inclined to agree with Christian thinkers such
as Herbert Butterfield and Reinhold Niebuhr, who have suggested that the Christian historian must learn to live with
moral obscurity and paradox, since both exist in great abun-
dance in the actions of man, and who have also noted that a
Christian approach to history, therefore, does not lead to
clear-cut or easy answers. The Bible says that "God's ways
are beyond finding out": the authors of the essays in this
volume believe that this tells the contemporary Christian
historian something about his limitations as an interpreter
of the past.

However, although the authors of these essays recognize
the limitations of the Christian historian and are aware that
they are "locked in a world of partial visions,"[11] they are nonetheless convinced that a Christian approach to history is both
possible and profitable. For though certainty concerning events
of the past is elusive, valuable things can be learned through
the study of history concerning God and man and the way
man ought to relate to his neighbor. There is no need to further elaborate at this point on the mediating approach to
Christianity and history, since this viewpoint is amply developed in the essays that follow. It is sufficient to say here
that the authors have attempted to avoid the tendency toward
pride that seems implicit in the stance of overassurance,
while at the same time eschewing the tendency toward over-
diffidence, which seems to verge on sloth.

IV

Despite this shared point of view, each author approaches
the question of the relationship of Christianity and history
in a somewhat different way, each considering to some extent
a different aspect of the problem. Two major types of approach are evident: the essays dealing with the relationship
of Christianity and history in a more or less general way

11. Butterfield, *Christianity and History* (New York, 1950), p. 118.

appear in Part I of the book, while specific critiques of the work of Christian scholars on the subject, as well as a bibliographical essay, appear in Part II. The book, therefore, moves gradually from the statement of general principles to more specific studies related to the question of a Christian approach to history.

The first two essays in Part I, " 'Why Study History?' Mused Clio," by Dirk W. Jellema, and "A Christian Perspective for the Teaching of History," by George M. Marsden, approach the question of the relationship of Christianity to history in the most general way. While Jellema is more Socratic and tentative and Marsden more direct, both wish to introduce some working principles that will be of use to Christians as they study or teach history. The remaining essays in this section relate general principles of Christian historiography to developments in modern historical scholarship. C. T. McIntire, for example, in "The Ongoing Task of Christian Historiography," after surveying the present state of historiography in North America as well as earlier efforts to develop a Christian historiography, suggests several areas in which he feels "contributions of Christian values and insights can be significant in the development of a further Christian historiography." Donald A. MacPhee, in "The Muse Meets the Master: Clio and Christ," follows a somewhat similar approach, reviewing recent developments, specifically in American historiography, and then suggesting several areas in which the Christian viewpoint on history may be related to these developments. In addition, MacPhee relates his Christian commitment to his teaching activities in a secular university. The final essay in Part I, "History as a Social Science: A Christian's Response," by Edwin J. Van Kley, considers from a Christian viewpoint some implications of the recent impact of the social sciences as they relate to the human values traditionally associated with the historian's vocation.

Part II of the book considers more directly some of the recent interpretations of Christianity and history that have provided the context in which the discussions in Part I take place. Three quite diverse types of approach are considered in detail. The work of Herbert Butterfield, who has probably shaped contemporary thought on the subject more than any other author, is considered by William A. Speck, whose analysis is informed in part by a lengthy interview with Butterfield himself. While Butterfield is a respected "secular historian" who related his faith to his learning, Professor Speck's other subject, Kenneth Scott Latourette, has reflected an approach more traditional among evangelical scholars. Working primarily in church history, he did not hesitate to point out the hand of God when he thought he saw it. Contrasted to the points of view of these two outstanding historians is that developed by the Dutch philosopher, Herman Dooyeweerd, whose evaluations of the meaning and significance of history are here analyzed by Dale K. Van Kley.

Finally, M. Howard Rienstra's bibliographical essay places the entire discussion in a wider context. His summary points out both the complexity of the issues that have been involved in recent discussions of Christianity and history, and brings some order to that complexity. Distinguishing among the respective concerns of historians, philosophers, and theologians, he identifies the major kinds of questions that lie behind the vast body of literature on the subject and suggests starting points for further reading on the issues.

"Why Study History?" Mused Clio

Dirk W. Jellema

Preamble

TO ATTEMPT a satisfactory treatment of a complex topic is to risk the difficulty of the proverbial carload of flatlanders, who while en route to Pittsburgh found themselves befogged, and emerged far up in the hills of West Virginia, tired and lost. They asked directions from an aged patriarch they encountered, and he, after five minutes of silent rumination punctuated with thoughtful ejections of chewing tobacco, issued the gloomy and emphatic rejoinder: "There ain't *no* way to get to Pittsburgh from here."

Similarly, there seems no way to cover our subject adequately and briefly. Further, whatever way we take, there will be fog and rough terrain, and the trip is bound to be not very satisfactory. To keep to the analogy of the story, we may not even get to Pittsburgh. The difficulties start immediately.

Suppose we do hold to the analogy. Imagine a driver and his son and daughter, who while en route to Pittsburgh. . .

"Why Study History?"

The rejoinder of the aged hillman produced merely giggles from Tina and guffaws from Claude, once they were back in the car, but Mr. Driver was dismayed. He felt a migraine headache coming on, and the last of the aspirin was gone long ago. Perhaps a brief nap would help. "Why don't you and Claude explore the vicinity for five minutes," he said. "I'm going to cat-nap. But don't get out of sight of the car." He watched them get out, and then leaned back in the seat. At this rate, we'll arrive at least a day late, he thought to himself, and what will we do about church: we may still be lost in these miserable mountains. Oh, to be in Pittsburgh, with a soft bed, soft beds of ease . . . . . to dream of a soft bed of ease . . . . . to dream. . . . . .

Claude and Tina slammed the doors noisily as they came back in the car. "Let's go!" said Claude exuberantly. (He doesn't seem to realize the situation we're in, thought Mr. Driver resignedly.)

"Let's, like, move!" exclaimed Tina gaily.

Mr. Driver started the car and drove back down the road. The fog was getting thicker. After a pause, Claude cleared his throat. "Tina and I were talking about something in school that bothered us," he said.

"Fine, fine," replied Mr. Driver. "Let's discuss it. It will help pass the time."

"Well," said Claude, "Tina and I were wondering why we have to study history."

Tina agreed. "It's a question a lot of us have. Why study history?"

Mr. Driver replied, "Claude, I don't understand your question. Surely it is true that we as Christians must do everything we do for the glory of God. How do we do that? By following God's commands, by obeying His will. What is His will for us? That we love Him, and love our neighbor. It is simple." (But, he thought to himself, is it that simple? Wouldn't Claude and Tina raise more questions?)

Claude persevered. "Well, sure, but that isn't what I meant. Why study history *rather than doing other things*? There sure are other things that are more interesting!"

To Mr. Driver's annoyance, a chorus of shrieks, giggles and guffaws greeted this sally. Yet, on reflection, he realized that Claude's point was well taken. After all, it was true that no one had an infinite amount of time or energy: why, then, expend a valuable portion of it in studying history, rather than taking basket-weaving, or adding an additional chemistry course, or playing football?

"When taught well, history can be a very interesting thing," he responded, realizing immediately that this was an unprofitable gambit to pursue. "Furthermore, that is a good question that you raise, Claude."

His audience waited expectantly. Driver, sparring for time, considered saying, "The answer is that you should follow what your elders tell you to do," but dropped the idea quickly: Claude had raised a serious question.

In fact, thought Driver with increasing desperation, he had no ready answer for it. Was he now to make a fool of himself all the way to Pittsburgh? He thought momentarily of the gloomy patriarch with his chaw of tobacco: he at least had five minutes to consider his answer. Was there no way out of this absurd situation?

"LOOK OUT!" screamed Tina from the back seat.

Driver slammed on the brakes. There, looming ahead in the fog, was a hitchhiker, carrying a sign that said: *Christian Historian Hitchhiking.*

The Hitchhiker's Answer

"Pointer is the name," said the historian as he climbed into the car. "Been visiting my brother up the road. He's the one that always tells people that there ain't no way to —"

"Yes, yes, we know," said Driver hastily.

"Should have asked him how to get to Cincinnati," said Pointer, and chuckled obscurely in his beard. "You look perplexed, Driver. Been arguing religion with teen-agers?"

"Well, not exactly," said Driver evasively. "I was just trying to explain why a Christian should study history. Perhaps you could share with us your — "

"Simple!" said Pointer. "All things to the glory of God. That's the end of the matter."

"Yes, but why isn't that the beginning of questions, not the end?" asked Driver, wondering as he spoke where he had heard the phrase before. Claude?

"Oh, it is," replied Pointer. "It is. It is both."

This unexpected reply produced a brief and gloomy silence, and then Driver went on: "Why study history?"

Pointer interrupted, "Love God and love your neighbor. Simple."

But Driver was not satisfied. "I mean, why study history rather than doing something else? How does studying history teach us about God and how to love our neighbor more than would, say, studying chemistry, or making money, or playing football? As Claude said a while ago — "

Pointer at this moment sneezed loudly. "Must be this fog," he said. "Still thick in these hills. Good question. Two parts. First part first. How help know God. Simple. Part of God's revelation. *General* revelation. Not special: otherwise only Christians could know anything about history. Raises further problems. But. Part of God's revelation. Driver, you have a question. So does Claude. Same question. Claude?"

Claude, startled, took a moment to regain his mental footings. "But, uh, why study history rather than some other, uh, aspect of God's revelation, since we don't have time to study all of it anyhow?"

"Good," said Pointer. "Higher aspect. Reveals more. Man: crown of creation. History: study of man in society, acting through time. Reveals more." His voice suddenly shifted and he began intoning in a sonorous voice, "Rose-red Petra, half as old as time. Man, creation's crown, the very image and icon of the Word who made the far-flung suns, imagined before the abyss of time began. Though treasonous son, yet still the cupbearer of the King, the cup the King has filled. Shall they not through the journey down the long road build their mighty cities till the stars wane, shall not their songs echo through the cold lands of space till the King comes, shall not — " He sneezed again, and reverted to normal tones. "Crown of creation. Worth studying. Man in society, acting through time: at worst, surely one of revelation's high points. General."

Looking in the mirror, Driver noted that the back seat passengers showed looks of mixed puzzlement, enlightenment, and interest, as well as their usual congenital mulishness. He himself felt somewhat the same. Pointer seemed convincing, but curiously elusive for a man who started by saying it was all "Simple!" He resolved to pin him down. "We frequently hear of history as 'His Story.' Is that what you mean?"

"Precisely!" said Pointer vigorously.

Driver pressed on, for this was familiar ground: "Thus the student can see, in the working of history, many examples of the wonderful providence of God, frequently given in answer to the prayers of His people. For example, the great storm that scattered the Spanish Armada in 1588 — "

Pointer snorted indignantly. "Half-truths! Dangerous! Misleading! God sent the storm. But God sent the Armada! God sent Rome. But God made Rome fall. History is His

Story. Part of the Book of General Revelation. But that ain't no Dick-and-Jane primer! Idiotic idea." And Pointer banged on the dashboard.

Driver began to feel a slight throbbing in his temples: "But if that isn't the case, what specific moral lessons can the student learn from history?"

Pointer looked pained. "Already told you. No primer. Want specific moral lessons, find a primer. Nobody ever got a sense of revelation from Dick-and-Jane. Response to revelation is wonder and awe. Still, maybe . . . problem. Complex moral insights? Maybe. Probably. Niebuhr. Irony of history. Moral aspects of imperialism. Suchlike. Probably." And Pointer drifted into a semi-trance, occasional "Hmmm's" showing he was not asleep. After a moment of this, he roused himself: "Vietnam. Idiots!" And in a milder tone: "Sorry I jumped on you. Is a problem. Have to give a paper on it. Question, too, whether that's the historian's job. Maybe the theologian. Theologians should know history. Or the other way around. Anyway, complex moral insights, yes, probably."

Driver noted, with satisfaction, that Pointer was capable of some evasiveness also. On reflection, he thought he could follow Pointer's train of thought despite his cryptic style, and he also tended to agree with it, although he still sensed a certain vagueness and an aura of unsolved problems in Pointer's presentation. He resolved to raise further questions later, but a look in the mirror told him that both Claude and Tina seemed to have prior requests.

"I'm still not — " started Claude, but Tina's "Couldn't we go on to the second part of the question?" overrode whatever objection he had started; "I mean about how it can help us love our neighbor? I don't dig that at all."

History as Service

Pointer was not abashed. "Simple!" he said. "Love your neighbor. Means serve him. How serve him? Witness. How witness? Serve. How serve? Love." He peered slyly at Driver, but the question came rather from Claude: How could history help do this? To Driver's mild dismay, Pointer pulled out and lit a large and villainous-looking cigar, which he began to use to underline stages in his discourse.

"First. How serve neighbor: obviously, must *understand* him. And also yourself. To understand yourself and neighbor, you have to understand *man*. What better way than to study man in society through time? But that means studying *history*. Second. What barriers to such understanding, what blocks to understanding man, self, neighbor? *Provincialism*. The illusion that your own cultural town and its provincial standards are the only possible ones. Town may be big — USA. Twentieth century.

"Provincialism of place: USA standards taken as obvious. Even worse, provincialism of time. Idea that only 20th century standards are obvious. Unchristian! As though we through our works have gained special merit in the eyes of God! That we are obviously 'better' than Byzantium! As though — "

But here Claude, momentarily sensing a kindred anti-establishment feeling, blurted out, "Right on!"

"That's *not* what I meant!" said Pointer heatedly. "That's provincial too!"

"Could you give some examples of how such provincialism can affect our relations with our neighbors?" interposed Driver. He noted that his headache was now gone; perhaps it had gone over to Claude, or to Pointer.

"Surely! Everywhere! Trying to tell Buddhist monks in Vietnam who are dedicated to poverty that we're better because we make more refrigerators!"

"Right on," said Claude, softly, only to receive a glare from Pointer, who loudly continued:

"So-called students who mindlessly blow up buildings to try and change the system, not knowing anything about how systems have actually been changed in the past! People who think they know that African tribal culture must be inferior because it has fewer machines! People who — you help here, Driver. Ask them anything about black history."

Driver thought briefly, then asked when the first slaves were brought to America, receiving (as he expected) blank looks.

"There you are!" said Pointer, waving his cigar in triumph. "How can you help your black neighbor when you don't understand anything about *his* background and culture and values — his story — History!"

"And," said Driver, "the same applies to your neighbors in Quebec or Vietnam or England or anywhere."

Tina looked dismayed: "But why should we worry about all those people in Quebec — no, I guess we're not supposed to say that, if we're Christians." She looked more dismayed.

Claude looked still unconvinced, and Driver thought he could spot the next question. Claude obliged. "But why should we study all those dead and gone countries like Greece and Rome and Egypt? How does that help us to serve people today, in the 20th century?"

Driver thought it a good question, but remarked, "Mr. Pointer would say, Claude, that the phrasing of the question betrays something of the naive provincialism he was talking about. The question, however, still seems worth raising."

"Right on, Claude," said Pointer (thus earning a silent glare from both Claude and Tina). "Good question. Brings me to my *third point.*" He waved his cigar for emphasis. "Ties in with provincialism, too. Help your neighbor: what is it you're helping him deal with?" He looked expectantly at Claude, and then Tina, who finally replied:

"Well, I guess with his problems."

"Right! His *problems.* Of whatever sort — religious, cultural, economic, political, artistic. But how do we get an insight into how man's problems can be solved? By examining how different societies, widely separated in time and space, have dealt with the problems they faced, given the resources they had. These societies don't have to be *our* society in the USA, nor a society in the 20th century. In fact, they *ain't* going to be that much help" (Driver winced) "since they're the ones that *have* the problems we're trying to find out about solving." He turned to Driver, and in a different tone said, "Interesting point. Is history a science, and if so in what sense? Vague analogy here to experiment. Worth pursuin' sometime." He turned to Claude. "Give me a problem." Claude, by now intrigued, suggested "imperialism." Pointer turned to Driver, gesturing.

Driver thought a moment, and then asked Claude, "Do

you know how Rome tried to deal with the problems raised by its imperialism? Or England? Or which worked and which didn't? Or what problems were faced when the law and order of Roman imperialism vanished, and to what extent the solutions were successful?" He turned to Tina, "Same question: give a problem."

Tina reflected at some length. "I see the point. Whatever problem I bring up, you'll say that we have to look to history for approaches to an answer." Claude's silence gave assent.

Pointer looked pleased. "After all," he said, "I'm only a Pointer; you are the Drivers. So it's good that you think about things."

Driver, after a pause, announced again that perhaps they were nearing "beds of ease" in Pittsburgh, which produced an obscure chortle from Pointer. Then Driver said: "I'd like to raise another sort of question, maybe more theoretical." To his annoyance, Pointer chose this moment to sneeze loudly, blow his nose with emphasis, and announce that the fog was again getting thicker outside — and, as Driver looked ahead, indeed it was.

A Christian View of History

"What I'd like to ask," said Driver, "is whether there is a specifically Christian view of history, and if so, what it involves."

Pointer puffed angrily at his cigar. "Of course there is. Furthermore, that's what I've been talking about for the last two hours!"

"Yes," agreed Driver, "but in a rather general way. For example, does the Christian historian view history differently than other historians?"

"Yes and no!" replied Pointer, "and you know that yourself. In one sense, the Christian views *anything* differently. A Christian carpenter views carpentering differently than would an atheist carpenter. He knows the ultimate purpose of it, what goals it is to serve, why he is doing it. But in terms of sawing a board, he does the same thing that an atheist does.

And he may be a poorly trained carpenter, and do a worse job of sawing a board than the atheist would do."

Tina (who had been growing in sophistication during the long trip) broke in. "But if history is a complex form of revelation, isn't the analogy misleading, or incomplete? Aren't there other ways also?"

Pointer nodded slowly. "Yes — though this all gets rather sticky. In a negative sense, surely. But in *theory*, again. The Christian historian knows that man is complex, and thus *should* be free from simplistic explanations such as Marxism, Freudianism, extreme nationalism, naive evolutionism, and the like. He should tend to see history as a very complex thing, since he knows the complexity of man. Of course, in practice, he doesn't always do this. He, too, may take some simplistic view, for example, seeing history as a series of progressions towards the crown of history, our present American society. But it is true that he *should* be more free from such tendencies than one who is not a Christian."

Now Claude (also growing in sophistication) interrupted. "What about St. Augustine and his idea that the meaning of history is to be found in the story of the City of God?"

Pointer nodded. "Good question. Difficulty; who is in the City of God? But it's a possible approach. Toynbee, as you know, has something of the same sort of notion: the purpose of the rise and fall of civilizations is to produce the higher religions. Many problems, though."

Driver now recalled some of Pointer's earlier remarks. "Don't you feel," he said, "that such an approach really doesn't do justice to the notion of general revelation? That is, doesn't God reveal Himself not only in the sphere of church and religion narrowly conceived, but also in the whole process of the rise and fall of civilizations, or the development of societies, each with its own unique characteristics, each in its own way revealing something of God's infinite glory?"

Pointer waved his cigar enthusiastically. "It does seem to me that along those lines — " But he was interrupted.

"The fog really *is* lifting now," announced Tina, "and before we get to Pittsburgh I'd like to bring up something more practical. Like, how should history be *taught?*"

The Teaching of History

Annoyed at being stopped in mid-flight, Pointer stared grump-ily at her, and then brightened. "But that follows from what we've already said. You and Claude ought to be able to sum-marize it yourselves." There was a silence.

"Go ahead, Claude," encouraged Tina.

Claude cleared his throat, and then launched forth. "Any proposals for methods of teaching history depend, of course, on the underlying view of history held by the teacher, which is what we've been discussing. The following points would seem to be implied in the discussion. First, the purposes of teaching history are to give insight into God's revelation, and to aid us in showing love for our neighbor. Second, teaching should strive to avoid, and help the student avoid, provincial-ism of time and place. Third, the aim should be to instill not only factual knowledge, but also a sense of wonder, as well as aiding the ability to analyze and evaluate." He turned to Tina.

"Fourth," went on Tina smoothly, "teaching should con-sider all major components in man's efforts in society, and thus include not only political, but also religious, intellectual, economic, social and artistic developments, with the emphasis in a given case depending perhaps on the emphasis given by the society itself under study."

Pointer, listening closely, waved his cigar at Mr. Driver.

"Fifth," said Driver, "it would seem that a plausible teaching technique to gain our objectives might be to stress the problems faced by different societies (in various spheres: political, religious, and the like), and how they tried to cope with them, given the social and other resources they had available. Thus the student can gain some insight into the nature of such problems, and some insight as to alternative approaches to the solution of similar problems today."

"Sixth," said Pointer, waving his cigar, now down to a stub, "effective teaching involves getting into the given society under discussion 'from the inside' as much as possible. For the alternative approaches it takes involve not only its social, technological, and other resources, but also the values, the presuppositions and assumptions of the society. Two things, both need to be understood. On some issues, values make a difference. Example: what alternative evaluations of slavery might occur in Graeco-Roman culture and in a Christianized culture?" He gave a slight bow in Claude's direction.

"Seventh!" exclaimed Claude, "It would now seem to follow that a teaching methodology can be worked out in some detail. Thus, in dealing with the French Revolution, for example, the student would be asked to consider such things as: the intellectual presuppositions of supporters and opponents of it, the similarities and differences between it and other revolutions (the Puritan Revolution involved convinced Christians: what differences resulted?), the alternatives possible at various points in its development (could the Terror have been avoided? How?), the relation between revolution and reaction (after the defeat of Napoleon, why was the king brought back? Why not turn to democracy?), and so forth."

"Eighth!" announced Tina. "If the previous be granted, it follows that mere memorization of dates and events, besides being counter-productive in terms of student interest, can hardly be said to be 'teaching history.' The purpose of learning dates is merely to establish the chronological framework, the locations in time, which is only preliminary to any real 'teaching history.' To make memorization a goal in itself would seem to be pusillanimous pedagogical puffery, to say the least."

"Furthermore, and ninth," said Driver enthusiastically, "it follows that — "

But now Pointer interrupted vigorously. "I say, Driver, I think we're arriving at our destination."

The End of the Journey

"Fine! Jes' fine!" said Claude. "At last Pittsburgh with some ease and relaxation. Beds of ease, here we come!"

But Mr. Driver, who was gazing with increasing alarm at the highway ahead, was troubled. "This doesn't look like Pittsburgh!" he said in alarm.

Pointer banged on the dashboard in glee. "Of course it isn't, you idiots!" he shouted. "This is *Cincinnati!*"

Consternation reigned, for it was soon indubitably clear that such was indeed the case.

"How . . . but how can that be, Mr. Pointer!" exclaimed Tina. "I thought you were hitchhiking to Pittsburgh!"

Pointer laughed. "Of course not! You should have listened to what my brother said!" (All three Drivers suddenly remembered: there ain't *no* way. . . .) He added, more seriously, "No, my friends, on a journey like this, there ain't *no way* to find beds of ease! And that's what you intended to find in Pittsburgh!"

"But then," shouted Claude, "where were you hitchhiking to?"

Pointer looked at him smugly. "Cincinnati, of course!"

"But why?" asked Driver.

"Obvious!" rejoined Pointer. "I'm attending a convention of historians! I have to read a paper dealing with one aspect of the convention topic."

Driver felt his headache suddenly returning in full force. "What is the topic?" he asked, with a horrible feeling that he knew the answer.

"The Christian and History, naturally!" said Pointer. "Stop the car, Driver. This is downtown, and here's where I leave you."

"Don't go!" said Tina unexpectedly.

"I must," said Pointer.

"Tell me one thing before you leave," said Claude, seriously. "Once more. Why should we study history?"

Pointer looked at him, and Tina, and Mr. Driver. He too was serious. "Goodbye, dear friends. And you know the answer, which is the beginning of questions, and the end of questions. Alpha and Omega, beginning and end. Why? Because we must do all things . . . " — he pointed at Tina and Claude.

"For the glory of God," they replied soberly.

A tear, to Driver's amazement, flowed down Pointer's cheek. "Goodbye, dear friends," he said again, and stepped away into the busy downtown crowd.

"Wait!" cried Driver — but at that point the whole car began to shake violently.

And at that point Mr. Driver was rudely shaken awake.

Claude and Tina were shouting at him. "Wake up! It's time to get started! We have to get going to Pittsburgh!"

Mr. Driver looked confusedly around him. "Where did Pointer go? We can still catch him!" he shouted.

Claude and Tina looked puzzled. "You've been dreaming," said Tina. "Come on. We can't stay all day in the hills of West Virginia!"

Driver, still half in a daze, started the engine, and they set off down the highway. He noticed that fog was closing in.

After a pause of some duration, Claude cleared his throat. "You know, Tina and I were talking about a question at school that has us sort of bothered."

Driver stiffened upright in his seat. With a mounting sense of horror, he heard himself ask, "What is it, Claude? I'm sure we could discuss it."

"Well," said Claude, "it's, like, we were wondering why we have to study history. . . . "

A Christian Perspective for the Teaching of History

GEORGE M. MARSDEN

HISTORIANS are people who talk about what other people have done. Basically, it's as simple as that. There is no special language or complex methodology. The procedures for finding out what happened and talking about it are much the same as those that might be used in anyone's everyday experience.

A Christian's philosophy of history is therefore not essentially different from a Christian's philosophy of life. This is not to say that there is no Christian philosophy of history or that it makes little difference. Exactly the opposite is the case. Just as our Christian experience conditions the way we live every aspect of life, so it will condition our teaching of history. Of course, in some areas this difference will not be apparent. For instance, the Christian does not go about determining the date of the Declaration of Independence essentially differently from the non-Christian, just as in everyday affairs the Christian and the non-Christian will use basically identical procedures in determining the phone number of the local delicatessen. Nonetheless, as in daily life one's Christian commitment makes a crucial difference in every *important* decision, so whenever there are important decisions in the teaching of history a Christian perspective will make a substantial difference. In order to define that difference it will be useful for us first to consider the purpose that the Christian has for the study and the teaching of history.

The Christian Purpose in Teaching History

The basic reason why we who are Christians should teach and learn history is so that we may better understand ourselves and our fellow men in relation to our own culture and to the world. Since the Christian's task is to live in this world

31

and to witness to the love of God as manifested in Christ, it is essential for us to understand ourselves and the world as well as we possibly can. Love is the Christian's central obligation, and understanding is an essential ingredient in love. If we are going to love others, it seems evident that we should try our best to understand them. Somewhat less obvious, perhaps, is that understanding ourselves is an essential aspect of love. Self-centeredness is, after all, the opposite of love. We each naturally tend to build for ourselves an imaginary universe in which we reign at the center. Such self-centered universe-building is part of our natural tendency to pretend to be as God, or to think too highly of ourselves. The Christian experience, the experience of knowing God's love through the redemptive work of Christ, destroys our self-made, self-centered worlds. It gives us new perspective on ourselves; we see ourselves as creatures dependent on God. Our hearts are changed. We can no longer live as though we stand at the center of the universe; rather, seeing ourselves in the perspective where God is at the center of life, self-centeredness appears foolish and short-sighted and true love is possible.

How does this relate to history? First of all a Christian perspective on ourselves depends substantially on learning certain historical events revealed in Scripture. The historical documents collected in the Bible provide the record of God's acting in history, and it is in the context of those acts, centering in the death and resurrection of Christ, that we must view ourselves and our world. The prominence of historical events as the basis of our faith suggests that in the Christian world-view the past has profound significance. Christians who accept biblical revelation as an authoritative record of what God has done definitively to care for man's condition cannot absolutize either the prevailing standards of the present (as tends to be done in modern Western thought) or abstract absolutes (as was the tendency in Greek thought). One of the motifs in the philosophy of our civilization (among both moderns and Greeks) has been to regard the past as either relative or of little meaning. The Christian, on the other hand, must view himself as participating in an on-going active relationship between God and man in which the revelation of God's acts and will in the past provides continuing norms for creative responses to the present.

While biblical history contributes the most crucial perspective necessary for understanding ourselves and others, the rest of history (the teaching of which is the major concern of this essay) can help somewhat as well. If we better understand what other men and other cultures have done, we can contribute something toward reinforcing a perspective that will help destroy our self-made, self-centered worlds. With an historical perspective it will become much more difficult to believe that the world really revolves around ourselves or that the values and ideals of our culture and our era are the best there have ever been. C. S. Lewis has made one of the most eloquent statements of this point. Speaking to Oxford students in the autumn of 1939, just after the Second World War had broken out, Lewis asked whether the pursuit of learning during wartime was not akin to fiddling while Rome burned. In answering that even in such emergencies academic pursuits were invaluable, the British literary scholar emphasized particularly the study of history. "Most of all," he said,

> we need intimate knowledge of the past. Not that the past has any magic about it, but because we cannot study the future, and yet need something to set against the present, to remind us that the basic assumptions have been quite different in different periods and that much which seems certain to the uneducated is merely temporary fashion. A man who has lived in many places is not likely to be deceived by the local errors of his native village: the scholar has lived in many times and is therefore in some degree immune from the great cataract of nonsense that pours from the press and the microphone of his own age.[1]

Surely Christians should be most enthusiastic for the study of history with such a purpose. As Lewis suggests, history is of major importance in alerting us to the transitory character of many of the values of our own age and culture. Rather than unknowingly allowing our values to be conformed to passing contemporary standards, we can strive to evaluate our

1. C. S. Lewis, "Learning in War-Time," *The Weight of Glory and Other Addresses* (Grand Rapids, 1965), pp. 50-51.

current cultural norms intelligently and to apply to them the transforming values of Christ.

Although for the Christian the most compelling purpose for studying or teaching history is to gain such a perspective that contributes directly to Christian living, every human society requires some knowledge of history for another essential purpose — *memory*. If you, for instance, were to fall asleep while reading this essay and to wake up an hour later with no memory whatsoever, you would be virtually unable to function. Similarly, if the race of man lacked a memory, human society would be impossible. The point is obvious. Less apparent perhaps is that a memory which was too complete would be almost as debilitating as no memory at all. Suppose, for instance, that when you awoke from the slumbers that this essay might inspire, you found that you remembered everything that you had ever seen or learned — all the shopping lists, telephone poles, TV commercials, phone numbers, history books, etc., etc., etc. It would be nearly impossible to function. Life is much more tolerable with our relatively poor memories that, for all their faults, at least try to select for us what is important enough to remember. This necessarily selective character of memory illuminates an essential aspect of historical study. History, quite evidently, would be nearly useless if it attempted the impossible task of collecting all the facts of human experience, storing them perhaps in a giant computer. Even the much less ambitious task of collecting the most significant facts of history into an encyclopedia is of rather limited value. Almost every teacher of history gives assent to this principle that history is not merely a collection of facts. Yet in practice it often proves easier to teach history as a giant compilation of textbook facts, names, and dates. The result is that some teachers of history unwittingly seem to adopt as their model the programming of a computer, or perhaps of creating human encyclopedias that could be displayed on high school or college quiz bowl programs. Certainly learning essential facts provides the necessary framework for historical understanding; but just as surely the mere memory of historical facts as though that were an end in itself is not among the purposes of teaching history. The memory that history provides must be a *meaningful* memory. What distinguishes the historian from the chronicler, the encyclopedist, or the computer programmer is that the historian provides *interpretation* as part of memory. Interpretation is the primary job of the teacher of history. And if interpretation is the central aspect of our task, then it is clear that our Christian values are going to make an immense difference in the interpretations we offer.

How is a Christian's History Different?

1. *Selecting the Facts.* Whether one is a teacher of history or an historical researcher, and whether one is a Christian or something else, his value-system plays a crucial role as soon as he begins to attempt to look at "the facts." Although facts no doubt have an objective reality, we never encounter them except as part of our own subjective experience. Hence we do not deal with facts purely objectively, but always in the context of our own experience and of the general meanings we see in things. So, for example, the Christian views all objects as created by God, whereas the non-Christian does not. In the cases of most types of historical judgments this element of subjectivity makes little practical difference. The statement "Washington crossed the Delaware" would be equally true if made by the Christian or the non-Christian, and it seems to make little *practical* difference if the Christian believes that rivers, boats, and men are created by God so far as making this statement of historical fact is concerned. In some cases, however, our Christian point of view in perceiving facts may make substantial differences that will affect our subsequent interpretations. For instance the Christian, in contrast to many non-Christians, will not view man as merely a high-order animal with no ultimate moral responsibilities. Accordingly when the Christian encounters "the facts" concerning Washington's crossing the Delaware, his perception will include the recognition that these facts have some relationship to God's moral order. The precise character of that relationship will be a question of interpretation; yet the perception of such a relationship significantly separates the Christian's initial view of the facts from the perceptions of most of his non-Christian colleagues.

Despite any such differences in our perceptions about facts, the basic store of available information is the same for the Christian and the non-Christian, and both must use the most scientific and honest procedures for determining what the actual facts might be. However, again at this point the subjective differences between Christians and non-Christians come in. Because the Christian and the non-Christian have differing value systems and differing purposes for studying history, the facts in which they will be interested will differ as well. Such differences of interests among historians are universal. The native Tibetan historian will talk about many facts in his "History of the World" course that would be omitted by a native American teaching a course with the same title. Similarly the American historian whose value-system leads him to adopt an economic interpretation of history will emphasize many facts that will be neglected by his fellow American historian who is disposed to see intellectual factors as primary. So the Christian historian will talk about some facts that will be missing in courses taught by Marxist historians. For instance, the Christian historian would not systematically omit or subordinate the influences of Protestant Christianity in American history in the way that many public school textbooks do. Because of his own religious concerns, the Christian is more interested in questions of religious commitment than is the non-Christian. He might, for example, find it relevant to spend substantial course time speaking of the religious views of Pascal, whereas some non-Christian teachers or texts would find it more important to emphasize those facts about Pascal that suggest that he was primarily a precursor of the secular Enlightenment.

To say that one's Christian value-system makes a difference even in the facts that he chooses to talk about, is not to say that the Christian should distort history in order to exalt his own tradition. Because every historian has both a point of view and a purpose, some partisan distortion is inevitable in the process of selection. Yet despite the inevitability of bias, an historian should continually compensate for such tendencies with a degree of detachment that will permit him to weigh all available evidence and to present a balanced account of what happened even if it does not readily fit his preconceptions or prejudices. If, for example, he chooses to point out that evangelical Christians held the leadership in many of the nineteenth-century antislavery movements, he has an equal obligation to point out that many slaveholders used Christianity as a primary justification for slavery. Such balance and integrity is a prerequisite for a Christian historian both in gathering evidence and in the larger task of which selecting the facts is a part — interpretation.

2. *Interpretation.* Everything we have said thus far is preliminary to this crucial question: How does the Christian interpret the past differently from the non-Christian? At the outset we observed that just as our Christian commitment will affect every aspect of our lives, so also it will pervasively influence our approach to history. This is particularly true with regard to interpretation, which is the heart of our historical enterprise. Probably most Christians who have dealt seriously with this question would agree that our Christian perspective will greatly influence our interpretation of history. Christian historians, however, have disagreed considerably among themselves as to what precisely that influence will be. Some say that the influence is, and should be, largely implicit and unstated. Others argue that we should develop a comprehensive Christian philosophy that will provide detailed normative principles that can be applied explicitly to nearly all of our interpretive judgments. This essay will suggest some answers that lie between these two extremes. Our Christian interpretations should be explicit as well as implicit; there is little reason that we should not state directly and clearly what we are trying to do. Yet at the same time we must not make the mistake of supposing that because we are Christian we have all the answers. Much of what we may say in applying our Christian view of history must be tentative, since after all even on the most basic of Christian principles — Christian love — "we see through a glass, darkly." Nevertheless, we can see some things, even though imperfectly. Through God's revelation, we can have some certainty on various matters, and that knowledge inevitably influences our view of history. Consideration of the character of that influence may be divided into four categories, the first related to what Christians know

about the workings of God, the second to what they know about the nature of man, the third concerning human motivations, and the fourth (not entirely separable from the other three) related to value judgments and moral judgments.

A. Our Knowledge of God's Actions in History

We know first of all that God is our creator and that he acts in history. He is not merely a first principle or a transcendent abstraction, but a personal God who has decisively entered into and changed human history. We know of God's actions particularly in the history of redemption recorded in Scripture and centering in Christ. We know also that God will continue his redemptive work through the workings of the Holy Spirit in the church, and hence that the highest value and the most meaningful experience for men is knowing and loving God. We know also that human history will end in judgment. We can say therefore that there is meaning in the most fundamental developments in history and that there is a general progression defined by the actions of God in our history. However, to say that there is meaningful general progression does not necessarily mean that there is steady progress (in the sense of improvement). Men's own sinful actions often work against the purposes of God. We cannot say with any assurance, therefore, that the world is generally getting better (an implicit assumption in almost all standard histories, which almost always glorify change); nor can we assume that things are generally getting worse. All we do know is that God has worked in our history and is continuing to work, but outside of biblical revelation we do not know clearly his precise purposes in permitting particular historical developments.

Nevertheless, since the revealed evidence of God's workings in history does provide the context for our historical study, and since our knowledge of this redemptive context is so obviously central to our distinctly Christian view of things, traditional Christian views of history have tended to allow such knowledge about God to overshadow all other considerations. In the past, and to some extent still today, Christian historians have often suggested that our knowledge of biblical revelation gives us a precise interpretation of all of history.

The starting point for this argument is the general principle that all things are under the providence of God. From this valid observation it is an easy step to one that does not necessarily follow, that we know specifically how God providentially influences history. Here the Old Testament provides the most plausible model: God visibly blesses men and nations who serve him and punishes those who do not. The result is an apparently Christian view of history, which in its least elegant form designates it as "His Story" or the workings of God's providence. Thus the lessons of history become largely the readings of the special providences of God. So, for instance, most Protestants read the defeat of the Spanish Armada as God's direct judgment on Roman Catholic Spain. Roman Catholics, on the other hand, saw the Saint Bartholomew's day massacre of 1572 as God's direct judgment on the many "apostate" French Protestants who were slaughtered. Similarly, both sides in the American Civil War saw their victories as evidence of God's intervention in the cause of justice. So also some Christian historians today may suggest that the fall of the Third Reich is evidence of God's judgment on totalitarian crimes, though they fail to explain why other equally reprehensible dictatorships have continued to succeed in the twentieth century.

This traditional approach to Christian history contains several major weaknesses. First of all, it seems to involve the presumption that we can read the mind of God, that we can tell what God's purposes are in particular historical events. Closely related is an apparent failure to distinguish adequately between God's special revelation in Scripture and his more general revelation elsewhere. Biblical history records not only *that* God acts, but often tells us explicitly *how* and *why* God acts. Non-biblical historical records lack these latter qualities. At best we know only the most general principles of how God is working in historical developments. We must therefore exercise the utmost caution in our interpretations, lest we appear to be claiming special prophetic insights into the workings of God. Finally, as Professor Charles J. Miller has pointed out, any attempt to apply the patterns of Old Testament history to the era since the coming of Christ confuses the character of the two eras. In the Old Testament, God's care for his people involved direct material blessings as well as spiritual blessings. The New Testament age, on the other hand, is the age of the Spirit, when Christians are not told that they should expect to prosper in this world, but rather that they should expect to be the poor and the suffering.[2] Similarly, national distinctions are no longer the basis for blessings and curses as in the Old Testament. Rather it is an age when there is neither Jew nor Greek. We therefore cannot presume to correlate the judgments of God with a nation's apparent good or bad deeds.

Although we have stated that our knowledge of the general principles of God's working in history provides the essential context for our historical study and that it gives us assurance that there *is* meaning and progression, our analysis of the application of these principles to specific historical interpretations has turned out to be largely negative. Because of such negative considerations, some Christian historians and teachers have stopped here. Having seen the abuses to which some traditional Christian interpretations have led, they have reacted to the point of saying that the Christian historian does little that is different from the non-Christian, and that our primary obligation is simply to do our jobs honestly and well. They argue correctly that after all our job as historians is not to write the history of God, but the history of men. However, since talking about men is our task, there is much that the Christian knows concerning the nature of man that will provide positive insights in a Christian's interpretation of history.

B. Man: The Crown of Creation and the Self-Deceiver

Perhaps most striking of the insights on human nature that Christians have is the biblical revelation of the paradoxical character of man. On the one hand, man is the crown of creation, made in God's own image, and given both responsibility and capability to subdue the earth. On the other hand, man is fallen and is the great self-deceiver, constantly prone

2. Charles J. Miller, "Is There a Christian Approach to History?" *Fides et Historia*, II, 1 (Fall, 1969), 6-7.

to think more highly of himself than he ought.[3] Capable of great accomplishments, he tends to suppose that he needs no one else. Not seeing himself in the proper perspective as a creature whose greatest fulfillment is to serve his creator, the very cultural achievements that should make him great and give him proper self-respect are rather turned into sources of arrogance. Capable of formulating useful laws to describe and partially control the natural world, and capable of formulating laws for society that are temporarily viable, man tends to view himself as autonomous, a law unto himself. Capable of love, man is constantly in search of ways to vindicate his essential selfishness. Capable of the joys of true religion, man's pride and selfishness make him too shortsighted to accept God's gifts of love, and he is constantly building his own religions.

The Christian historian, with such knowledge that man is capable of being both the crown and the scum of the universe, views man's cultural achievements in this perspective. He therefore recognizes both the genuine values of the accomplishments of the race, but also points out how these same accomplishments form the bases for man's self-centered view of the world, and for his self-deceptive false religions.

A good example of how such a Christian perspective might work can be found in a Christian's interpretation of the Enlightenment of the seventeenth and eighteenth centuries. On the one hand, he may laud the great achievements of man's intellect and ingenuity during that era. Surely there was general improvement and benefit to man (all else being equal) in the increased understanding of the principles that governed the physical world, and in the ending of many of the erroneous and sometimes superstitious beliefs that were common in the pre-scientific era. Surely also there was genuine improvement and benefit in the technological achievements of that era that relieved men of some of their physical burdens. Certainly many men of oppressed classes benefited

3. The relation of these themes to history is developed in a most useful way in the works of Reinhold Niebuhr. For examples, see especially *The Irony of American History* (New York, 1952) and *Faith and History* (New York, 1949). My own interpretation of such themes reflects a Reformed theological tradition.

greatly by the effective attacks during that era on unwarranted privilege and unjust custom. Yet, while many false beliefs and practices were discarded, these same laudable achievements led many men to adopt new false religions. Having thought that they had discovered comprehensive natural laws for the physical universe, many men began to act as though they could retire God to the edge of creation as a sort of impersonal first cause. In many respects Enlightenment men were de-Christianizing thought, giving little attention to God's personal and active participation in the affairs of the world. Using as their model the laws for the physical universe, men in this era began to suppose that they could discover definitive natural laws for other areas of life as well. Only reason and a careful application of the scientific method seemed necessary to produce a society that would run as smoothly as the most sophisticated technological machine of the age. With such rational scientific principles, laws of morality could be discovered that would eliminate injustice. Man and society could be perfected, and progress toward a secular millennium could be assured. Many of these assumptions in modified form have continued to affect us in our own era. During the Enlightenment man had found new and dramatically effective ways to convince himself that he was his own authority. He had, in fact, created a new religion where man was God, reason and science were his revelation, and laws were of his own making. So the best achievements of the Enlightenment were often turned into the worst.

Man-made culture religions of this sort — that is, sets of man-made values and highest commitments that function as the operative religions of a culture — provide a constantly recurring theme in historical development. In earlier eras they often were embellished by the creation of an explicit claim to divine sanction, as rulers in many ages and cultures claimed divine right, or even to be divine themselves. In the modern era similar essentially religious commitments have less often involved explicit theistic claims. They have functioned as religions, nonetheless, and the historian may legitimately point this out. In the last two centuries, for instance, nationalism has been one of the most prominent of man's religions. For many it has taken on the essentially religious quality of ultimate allegiance to a higher power. As with a supernatural religion, many men have come to think of their nation as both a force to fear and as their ultimate source of security. Unlike some other culture religions, nationalism involves many of the specific external marks of religion. Like the Christian church, it is often founded on explicit creeds or ideology. It includes a set of moral values that condemns those who violate nationalistic mores. It even includes rituals, national anthems, and solemn ceremonies equivalent to hymns and liturgies. Like the Roman Catholic Church, which has the symbol of the cross to be venerated by crossing oneself, nations have flags to be venerated and saluted in a similar fashion. Nations even have an eschatology, promising people the hope of a better life in the future. While the Christian will readily acknowledge the proper place of patriotism, loyalty, and respect for the powers that be, and while he may point out some valuable results of nationalism, he may also indicate in his historical interpretation how these proper things have often been turned into false religions. A similar case can easily be made to show that Marxism, for instance, is also essentially a religious commitment, with saints, creeds, a millennium, etc. Although less explicit, faith in material prosperity, technology, scientific discovery, philosophy, and other intellectual achievements, almost all of which have brought vast benefits, have also frequently been turned into highest sources of value or security, that is, into man-made religions.

Such a general exposé of man's false religions could easily turn history into a very partisan and party-line affair. It could have a negative and self-defeating effect, for instance, if in the classroom the dominant impression created is that history is a contest of good guys versus bad guys, good ideas versus bad ideas, Christians versus lions. Although explicit interpretive stances are necessary, too much partisanship will often arouse suspicions. And rightly so. Teachers could easily ride a theme such as man's false religions to the point of constantly reiterating it even when it is so obvious that it need not be stated. It could then appear as a prejudice used as a substitute for interpretation. The antidote to such abuse is to remind ourselves of the primary purpose for emphasizing such a theme. Our purpose in studying history is not primarily to condemn others who have made mistakes, but rather to understand ourselves in relation to others and to culture. We study cultural values both because we want to understand those who hold them, and in order to understand how these very ideas and assumptions have influenced us. Christians are seldom if ever immune from the cultural values of their age, and they constantly are in danger of equating Christianity with contemporary ideals. Analysis of the sources of the ideals of our culture can therefore be an extremely useful means of understanding ourselves and our own untested assumptions, which may be products of cultural influences more than Christian commitment.

In this important task of exposing untested assumptions that shape us and our culture, the role of the historian is analogous to that of the psychoanalyst. In somewhat the same way that unconscious and subconscious factors influence our psychological development, deep-seated cultural patterns, ideals, values, and assumptions exert a subtle and often unrecognized influence on everyone in that culture. To the extent that these influences remain unconscious we are controlled by them; but to the extent that we are made conscious of these influences we are in a position to discriminate among them and to exercise a degree of control over them. So, as the analyst brings unconscious psychological factors into consciousness by tracing their roots back to their childhood origins, the historian brings cultural patterns, ideals, values, and assumptions to consciousness by tracing them back to their historical origins. If only the present is considered, current political and social patterns, as well as general cultural ideals, often appear to have a certain inevitability about them. Once it is seen, however, how these patterns or ideals developed, who first formulated them, what preceded them, and what were the alternatives, they lose that illusion of inevitability and it is possible not only to understand them better but also to discriminate among them according to Christian principles.

A closely related aspect of uncovering man's self-deceptions is the exposure of truth and error in popular mythologies. Here the historian's job is largely a matter of setting the record straight. Every culture and era is filled with popular beliefs, political slogans, and the like that involve historical interpretations. For instance, for many centuries, including most of our own, substantial numbers of people in all Western nations believed that there was an "International Jewish Conspiracy." Similar mythologies have often developed about the superiority of one race or nation, or suggested that a particular racial group, interest group, or ideological affiliation has had a monopoly on aggression and war-making. Other popular mythologies have been based on false historical analogies. The disastrous peace pact at Munich, for instance, has been used ever since as a justification for settling conflicts militarily. Only slightly different are the types of mythologies that have often led nations to "fight ghosts," on the assumption that somehow history generally repeats itself. So, for instance, in Europe after 1815 men on one side of the political spectrum worked with great passion to prevent a recurrence of the French Revolution of 1789, while on the other side men worked with equal passion against the return of the *ancien régime*, even though the conditions for those eighteenth-century phenomena were unrepeatable.[4] Similar "ghosts" can be found in every era. The Christian historian, like the non-Christian, does valuable service if he does no more than to clear the minds of his audience of some of the nonsense of the slogans and mythologies of his era.

C. Human Motivation

The historian's view of human nature often plays a decisive role in describing men's motives, another area where the historian must frequently make interpretive judgments. "What *really* caused men to act the way they did," the historian often finds himself asking. "Was it ideology, economic interests, social pressures, class conflict, identity crises, unconscious psychological forces, etc.?" Frequently, historians choose one such factor as being the primary motivating factor in human action, and in doing so they are implicitly reflecting their own views of human nature. Since the Christian enjoys some

4. This concept and the illustration of it are from Sir Lewis Namier, "History," in *The Varieties of History,* ed. Fritz Stern (Cleveland, 1956), p. 373.

light of revelation concerning the character of man, we would expect our Christian views to affect such judgments.

They do so in two ways. The most obvious is that among the factors that the Christian allows as possible causal explanations are genuine supernatural events where God acts in history. Such factors are crucial in our interpretation of the miraculous events in biblical history. They are also admitted as possible explanations in later eras in that the Christian recognizes the continuing active work of the Holy Spirit, particularly in effecting genuine changes of heart that are fundamental factors in human motivation. Even in such cases, however, the genuineness of a man's religious profession may be quite difficult to determine. Furthermore, in cases where we suspect the operation of spiritual factors, other causal factors are by no means excluded from our explanations. The Holy Spirit, after all, often operates through secondary means, and the analyses of these mundane factors are far more in the province of the historian than is pronouncing on the presence of the Holy Spirit. For instance, in describing a conversion experience (such as that of Constantine or Luther) the Christian historian may be tentative about the validity of the experience, but he should also take into account other causal factors (such as the character of the era, the religious contacts of the convert, his psychological background, his education, the immediate crisis he may have been in, etc.). Regardless of whether the experience was valid, these were contributing causes and help explain why it happened.

The second way in which our Christian views affect our causal judgments is closely related, but more tentative. Even if nothing else were clear about the Christian view of man, it would be clear that it taught that man is very complex. In Scripture, examples of almost every sort of human motivation appear: sex, greed, lust for power, status anxiety, unconscious factors, avarice, nationalism, class struggle, faith, hope, love, commitment to ideals, and trust — to name only a few. Recognizing this fullness of the complexity of man, the Christian historian would be reluctant to accept one motivational factor as always primary (for example, class struggle). He would, however, be willing to exclude certain types of motivation as usually primary. Man's natural motivations, the

Christian knows from Scripture, are not generally benevolent or selfless. Rather, men since the Fall characteristically have been driven by sinful self-interest. The Christian historian accordingly could not consistently adopt a mode of interpretation that was basically optimistic about men's potential outside the work of God's grace.

D. Moral Judgments and Value Judgments

Since almost all historical interpretation involves moral judgments or value judgments, our consideration of this final topic is not entirely separable from what has been said thus far, and to some extent it will involve reiteration and summary. We have already observed that value judgments are always implicit even in our selection of facts. In interpretation, the pervasive place of such judgments is nearly self-evident. Using as our norms the standards of Christian moral and spiritual values, Christian historians will inevitably give more approval to some historical acts and events than to others. Constantly we will be making such judgments when we appraise man's cultural achievements or expose his culture religions. Continually we will be suggesting standards for human relationships of which we approve and those of which we disapprove. Repeatedly we will be presenting historical ideologies with which we agree or disagree.

Granting that such moral judgments and value judgments have an important and inevitable place, the most significant practical question for the Christian teacher is the extent to which he should make his judgments explicit or leave them implicit. Some Christian teachers appear to feel that every history lesson should have a moral. Such an approach can be self-defeating for two reasons. One is that it involves the danger of substituting moralism for more significant historical analysis. The second danger is that students may be turned off by such partisan Sunday-school tactics. On the other hand, other historians who desire to appear more professional may by way of reaction to the moralizers attempt to exclude explicit moral and value judgments. Since implicit judgments are being made anyway, such an approach involves an unnecessary lack of candor, and may suggest that the study of history is a detached academic exercise. Again, of course, the answer lies somewhere in the balance between these two extremes; precisely where it lies will vary according to particular teaching situations, academic levels, backgrounds of students, intellectual abilities, and skills of the teacher.

The whole problem of making moral judgments can perhaps be clarified somewhat by considering the character of the judgments which the Christian historian should characteristically present. While judgments of right or wrong concerning historical actions are proper, one must be careful to distinguish between such moral judgments in the sense of analysis and those in the sense of condemnation. Too often, moral judgments by Christians have the condemnatory quality; hence they appear obnoxious. To counteract this tendency, the Christian teacher must be careful to emphasize that the summary of Christian morality is not condemnation, but rather is love. Since love implies some sympathy for our fellow men, the moral judgments made in history must encourage such sympathy and understanding. Also, as was suggested earlier, we must always make it clear that the follies of men whom we study are in a sense our own follies as well. Profession of Christian faith in itself is no guarantee against such failings. In fact, it is helpful to remind ourselves that, as Reinhold Niebuhr observes, "the grossest forms of evil enter into history as schemes of redemption and . . . the Christian faith itself introduces new evils, whenever it pretends that the Christian life, individually or collectively, has achieved final perfection."[5]

In this regard, incidentally, a sense of humor (as well as a sense of humility) can be a teacher's most valuable asset. A sense of humor requires perspective on both ourselves and on others — sufficient perspective to see the incongruous. Both the Christian view of man and a sense of history encourage such perspective. They encourage a perspective that allows us to see the genuine humor, as well as the irony and tragedy, in the pretensions of men; but at the same time it allows us to laugh at ourselves and our own pretensions. In

5. Niebuhr, *Faith and History*, p. 214.

a Christian perspective we can see the incongruities and relative insignificance of some of our most cherished individual and cultural achievements. In history, as in life, there is a time to laugh. Without such humor, along with our fundamental goals of sympathy and understanding, it is nearly impossible to teach and to communicate the serious aspects of our Christian message.

Essentially, then, the same principles that apply to everyday life apply to our study and teaching of history. We talk about men — their accomplishments and their follies. We may praise them, or we may criticize them, we may even laugh at them. Inevitably we must evaluate their ideals and actions in terms of the revealed standards for man's proper relationship to God. Yet we must also consider them in terms of our proper relationship to our fellow men — as those who may differ from us yet have a great deal to say to us — as those who but for the grace of God are no different from ourselves — and as those whom we must attempt to understand and to love. With this perspective on others, we should also be gaining added perspective on ourselves. We should begin to be able to view our own accomplishments and follies in a perspective that will help destroy the illusion that we stand at the center of the universe.

The Ongoing Task of Christian Historiography

C. T. McIntire

The Task: A Christian Historiography

QUESTIONS about the nature and character of the historian's task are not commonplace among practicing historians in North America. So pervasive is the impact of positivism and liberal democratism upon historians that they do not often feel the need to reflect on the philosophical and methodological bases of their work. This is not to say that there is little published work in philosophy of history. On the contrary, publications on philosophy of history may be increasing in number, but the authors are often philosophers, especially from the school of linguistic analysis, or perhaps theologians, including the Bultmannians and some evangelicals who wonder about the relationship of the biblical accounts to history. Historians, as distinct from philosophers or theologians, as David Herbert Donald remarks, "avoid the philosophy of history mostly because it is of so little assistance to them in writing or teaching." At the Ph.D. level in the universities historical methodology is treated primarily as a matter of technique, while study of the philosophy of history has become virtually nonexistent.[1]

The neglect of the fundamental questions has become obvious in recent years because of the appearance in North America of serious neo-Marxist historiography. Historians such as Staughton Lynd, Eugene Genovese, and the participants in the Radical Caucus of the American Historical Association draw upon an immense Marxist and neo-Marxist tradition in Europe which includes such eminent practitioners as Christopher Hill and Eric Hobsbawm. The North

---

1. David Herbert Donald, "Between Science and Art," *American Historical Review*, LXXVII (1972), 445. The journal *History and Theory*, which besides its articles publishes special bibliographies on philosophy of history, is a good place to sample current discussion of the underlying issues of history.

American neo-Marxists have called attention to the existence of an amazing, uncritically accepted homogeneity or consensus dominant among historians. The consensus rests on certain leading convictions of a philosophical sort, chief among them being an obstinate resistance to any systematic reflection upon the fundamental questions of historical study. Two concomitant convictions are a belief in the neutrality, objectivity, and pragmatism of their way of doing history, and a devotion, however critical, to the values and necessities of liberal democratic society. The neo-Marxists, whose work creates the occasion for comparison, make possible the observation that the established positivist-liberal historiography, like their own, is indeed loaded with distinctive assumptions, values, and rules that are institutionalized in the universities and historical associations.[2] It becomes evident that all historians function with pretheoretical commitments, however unselfconscious they may be, which shape their research, method, teaching, and writing. I should emphasize that I refer to something more radical than mere personal bias, prejudice, narrowness of view, special pleading, or even unfairness.

This period of awareness of the fundamental questions in historical study can be viewed as an opportunity to clarify certain matters of importance to Christian historians. In one context there appear renewed tendencies among Christians from many traditions to regard their work, whatever it may be, as a calling within which to serve God and their fellow human beings. As the need becomes greater for more self-consciousness in implementing Christian motives, many Christians are enlarging their own awareness of questions of world-view and way of life. There are immediate implications of such renewal of Christian vision for Christian historians. In another context, certain characteristics of our age are gradually awakening among Christians a dissatisfaction with secular ways of doing things but without implying a disengagement from a full life in the world. We experience

2. The radical-liberal debate over history has extended to a battle within the American Historical Association, which was especially heated in 1968-1970. Some of the controversy is reflected in the *American Historical Review* and the *AHA Newsletter*.

perhaps a new phase in the age-old task of living in the City of God while we live within the City of Man. When Christian historians examine with sensitivity the convictions, values, and purposes of both the positivist-liberal historiography and the alternative neo-Marxist historiography, we may discover that, no matter how much we may rightly learn from them and whatever our dependence on them, our Christian perceptions of things are radically different from both. Likewise we may detect certain deadends or fundamentally unhelpful interpretations of history that Christian insight might help to reformulate. We may in this context be concerned with the question of a Christian historiography.

By the term Christian historiography I mean to convey something specific.[3] I use the word "historiography" to indicate that it has to do with the study and writing and perhaps the teaching of history as practiced by people whose profession is historian. I mean for it to address both the questions of the nature and meaning of history as well as of the nature of historical study and writing. The word "Christian" designates the identity and kinds of assumptions, values, understandings, and insights that underlie and implicitly characterize the historiography. Its starting points are alternative to the *a prioris* of other historiographies even while it interacts with and learns from them. Christian historiography refers not simply to history written by Christians, nor to historical studies of the church and theology, but to an historiography which itself examines the history of peoples, societal structures and institutions, ideas, mores, and patterns of life, according to the sorts of insights and values provided by a Christian view of people, society, norms, history, the world and the whole of created reality. Christian historiography means to enter into the study of history in such a way that it may lead to an analysis and account of the historical process that is true, insightful, and revealing of the human condi-

3. The essays and articles published elsewhere in this volume bring together some valuable pieces by historians which contribute to the discussion of Christian historiography. Two especially good essays that are to the best of my knowledge unpublished are W. Stanford Reid, "A Christian Understanding of History" (1970); and William W. Paul, "Cultural and Christian Presuppositions for the Interpretation of History" (1973).

tion and historical reality. Put still another way, Christian historiography involves self-conscious reflection on foundational things in order that the vocation of Christian historians may more readily be transformed by the motivation of the gospel and that the product of their labors may carry implicitly the marks of the gospel.

The Legacy of Christian Historiography

Given the assumptions of our age, the fact that there already exists a long history of Christian historiography is generally overlooked. It is as much a commentary on the power of secularism today as on the condition of Christianity that the practicing of a Christian historiography must now be advocated and not merely assumed as the work of Christian historians.

In many ways the place of Christians in academia today is not unlike that of early Christian thinkers amid the learning of the Greco-Roman world. R. G. Collingwood summarizes the point admirably:

> . . . when we find many of the fathers like Jerome, Ambrose, and even Augustine speaking of pagan learning and literature with contempt and hostility it is necessary to remind ourselves that this contempt arises not from lack of education or a barbarous indifference towards knowledge as such, but from the vigour with which these men were pursuing a new ideal of knowledge, working in the teeth of opposition for a reorientation of the entire structure of human thought.[4]

Christian scholars generally, including Christian historians, today have much the same task as then — a reorientation of the entire structure of human thought. But there is at least one crucial difference for Christian historians now: the "new paganism" of our age and in particular the prevailing positivist-liberal historiography and the neo-Marxist challenger have been unalterably shaped by the legacy of Christian historiography begun in the period of the Roman Empire. Collingwood continues his comment about the early Christian writers:

In the case of history . . . the reorientation not only suc-

4. R. G. Collingwood, *The Idea of History* (New York, 1946, 1956), p. 51.

ceeded at the time, but left its heritage as a permanent enrichment of historical thought.

Christian understanding of the nature of history radically transformed the conception of history and historical reality that prevailed in the Greek and Roman worlds. The writings and Christian perspectives of Sextus Julius Africanus, Eusebius of Caesaria, Orosius, and Augustine provided alternatives to the classical pagan views of Polybius, Plutarch, and Livy. Collingwood rightly calls this patristic product "Christian historiography." These Christian ideas entered into the presuppositional framework of Western civilization. Subsequent Christian historiography in the medieval period of the *Corpus Christianum* and in the sixteenth and seventeenth centuries of the Protestant and Catholic Reformations further contributed to building and refining the common framework of assumptions about history. The works of Cassiodorus, Gregory of Tours, Bede, Jean Froissart, Beza, and Bossuet — to name suggestively only a few over a vast twelve-hundred-year epoch—contributed in various ways to the decisive transformation of historical understanding by Christian historiography.[5]

It is not my purpose here to study the history of Christian historiography as such, although the need for such a study is evident. I am content to make the point that in our own century, historiography in the Western world depends in one manner or another upon certain common underlying convictions about the nature of history whose origins will be found in the legacy of Christian historiography. My point is as much one capable of confirmation in historiographical examination — in fact historically such convictions entered the Western lineage from Judaeo-Christian sources — as it is a product of intuitive recognition of originally Christian ideas that continue to function today, although in a radically transmogrified form as secular convictions. Some of these

5. Two important studies that provide helpful overviews of the history of historiography are James Westfall Thompson, with Bernard J. Holm, *A History of Historical Writing*, 2 vols. (New York, 1942; reprint, Gloucester, Mass., 1967), and Harry Elmer Barnes, *A History of Historical Writing*, 2nd ed. (New York, 1962). See also C. A. Patrides, *The Grand Design of God* (Toronto, 1973).

assumptions I can identify. They have to do with the larger questions of the direction and character of history.[6]

The assumption that historical time should be perceived as the past, the present, and the future, the far or near past or the far or near future, is so common to us that we forget that such a perception did not belong to the classical Greeks or the Romans. According to Collingwood, Greek historiography, with perhaps the exception of Herodotus, worked with the notion of timeless permanence as the important reality behind the ephemeral horizon of change we know in human life. Moreover, this temporal horizon was regarded as having a rhythm of repetition on the model of the physical universe so that human life may expect to experience a recurrence of typical events. By the time of Livy, in Roman historiography, these tendencies of the Greeks to regard reality as timeless on one hand and recurring on another were fully developed. Livy's history of Rome demonstrates the problem. Collingwood writes: "[For Livy] Rome is a substance, changeless and eternal. From the beginning of the narrative Rome is ready-made and complete."[7]

The perspective of past-present-future is a Hebrew and Christian supposition. In the view of the biblical Jews, the Exodus from Egypt happened one time in the past to their forefathers. It was succeeded by other events including their migration into the territory of Canaan, their battles with certain opponents, their neglect of the worship of God, the kingship of David. Jesus, Luke, and Paul clearly understood this perspective of historical time as well. Moreover, both the Jews and Christians looked forward to the future, to the coming Messiah for the Jews and to the second coming of Christ for the Christians. These awaited events of the future defined the horizon within which their lives were understood.[8] The

6. See two helpful articles by W. Taylor Stevenson, "Christian Faith and Historical Studies," *Faith and Learning Studies*, II (New York, 1964); and "Theology and History: The Relations Reconsidered," *The Christian Scholar*, XLVI (1963).

7. Collingwood, pp. 14-45.

8. Psalm 78 can serve to illustrate the Jewish notion of the past, and Zechariah 7 and 8 and Revelation illustrate the horizon of the future. See the comparisons between Greek and Christian ideas of time and history in Oscar Cullmann, *Christ and Time: The Primitive Christian Conception of Time and History*, trans. Floyd V. Filson (Philadelphia,

patristic writers adopted this understanding of historical time.

The notion of periodization, essential to all historiography today, followed from this. The biblical Jews and Christians marked epochs by the criterion of significant events — the journey of Abraham, the Exodus, the building of the temple in Jerusalem, the exile into Babylon, the birth of Christ, the death and resurrection of Christ, the conversion of Paul, the second coming of Christ. The Christian historiography of the patristic, medieval, and Protestant and Catholic Reformation eras continued to work with periodization on the biblical model.

The understanding of history as a process is also allied to the Judaeo-Christian perception of historical time. In the biblical accounts history is viewed as an ultimately unbroken, unified movement of affairs and events in a direction from the former state of things, the beginning, toward the consummation of all things in the apocalyptic events, the eschaton. All of history is embraced within this directional process of events. However the nature of this historical process may be construed by historians of our own century — whether as a cultural evolutionary phenomenon on the analogy of biology, or as a progression of class struggle toward the liberation of the oppressed, or as the progressive moral amelioration of humankind, or even as a succession of chance occurrences — the basis of these secular construals remains the Judaeo-Christian idea of historical process toward the eschaton.[9]

With the appearance of the Christian ecclesia came a break with the self-centered particularism of both the ancient Near Eastern and the Greek-Roman worlds. Christianity implied in principle an opening up of the horizon of historical experience to the whole of mankind. In the Christian view, God's affairs embrace all peoples and the gospel is able to transform all human cultures. This historical universality

---

1950); Reinhold Niebuhr, *Faith and History: A Comparison of Christian and Modern Views of History* (New York, 1949). On Luke and biblical history, see I. Howard Marshall, *Luke: Historian and Theologian* (Exeter, 1970).

9. I should emphasize that "process" does not mean "progress." The conviction that the historical process was also one of human progress is a secular post-Renaissance one. See Niebuhr on this, *passim*, but especially chapters 1, 2 and 5.

makes even the expansive Roman Empire look partial by contrast. Thereafter, in Christian historiography, the affairs of
one people had to be viewed in ultimate conjunction with all
other peoples, and all in relation to God's total provision for
humankind. In the medieval and Reformation eras and after-
wards this notion stimulated the writing of what was called
for a while "universal history." Today we speak of world
history.

These Christian ideas decisively contributed to the notion of historical contextuality. Each event in the biblical
accounts — the Exodus from Egypt, for example — was
viewed in relation to other events and to the whole process
of history as God implemented his provision for his people,
for humanity, for the whole creation. In the Christian era
events were related contextually as well to the universality
of God's work with humankind.

One of the most crucial contributions of biblical and
early Christian historiography was its understanding of human
beings as the makers of history. Greek historiography realized
that the subject matter of history was human activity, rather
than that of the gods, but defined the human position in history as merely that of a rational animal capable of acting on
the basis of rational willing. This idea, when joined with the
notions of permanent substances and recurrent, ephemeral,
temporal change, actually had the effect of circumscribing
the human role in history.[10] By contrast, the biblical accounts
depicted human beings as much more full and complex persons than merely rational beings and as the very ones for
whom God made the whole creation. Human beings as the
centrum of the creation were, in the Judaeo-Christian vision,
understood as culture-creators entrusted with the monu-
mental yet everyday task of superintending and unfolding the
creation. Humans in the biblical accounts were regarded as
next to God himself, made in the image of God, and given
the decisive role in working out the well-being of the whole
creation. This Christian view of human beings as makers of
history and creators of culture went far beyond the Greek
view of humans in history. Of course, the version of this bib-

10. Collingwood, pp. 40-42. My view here differs from the conclusions
Collingwood comes to about Greek "humanism."

lical understanding of men and women that remains operative in much of today's historiography has been translated by Enlightenment and Victorian perceptions of progress into a secular humanism, however much it may be circumscribed by the doubts about human capacity raised by existentialism, behaviorism, certain deterministic trends in Marxism, and by the shock of war, economic depression, and environmental deterioration.

Still another crucial legacy of biblical and Christian historiography was the conviction that the whole of the diversity and complexity of reality fitted together into a coherent totality, and that everything within it, each event, as well as the whole of reality and human history, is meaningful. In the Christian version it is God through Christ who is the source and maintainer of the wholeness of reality and its meaning. In the secular versions of the Christian idea, the coherence and meaning of reality may be called into question or misunderstood through faulty human perception, for example, by treating historical reality as if it were a matter of chance, or claiming that the historian is the source of coherence. Nevertheless, however atrophied it may be, some presupposition of the coherence and meaningfulness of historical reality *de facto* underlies modern historiography. Without it, the possibility of historical study's being worthwhile or telling something true is vitiated.

Much more could be said to indicate the legacy of Christian historiography from the biblical, early Christian, medieval, and Protestant and Catholic Reformation eras. I am content to underscore the centrality of these few Christian assumptions, however secularized they may have become, about historical time, periodization, the process character of history, the universality of history, historical contextuality, human beings as the makers and creators of history, and the coherence and meaningfulness of reality, including historical reality. These ideas underlie the configuration of assumptions common to much historiography today.

More Recent Christian Historiography

Christian historiography did not cease with the early modern era. Much of the important historical writing in the eighteenth and early nineteenth centuries could be classified as Christian. Two trends in the eighteenth century, developed during the nineteenth, and crucial to the history of Western civilization itself, radically transformed the character of Christian historiography and its place in the context of historical study. First was the development of scholarly or scientific study itself, including historical study. Historical study gradually became distinguished from philosophy, or theology, or literature, or law, while historical writing gradually became distinct from holy biography, moral tale, memoir, chronicle, and polemic. It was refounded on disciplined analysis and archival and documentary research. Christian historiography both contributed to and benefited from this general development of the systematic structure of historiography. The work of the historian Leopold von Ranke on German history and the papacy will illustrate how indispensable one eminent Christian was to this process.[11]

The second trend, upon which the first partially depended, was the secularization of Western society and with it the secularization of scholarly or scientific study, including historical study. I refer not simply to the gradual cessation of ecclesiastical or theological control over historical study. More important to my theme is the emergence of a new spirit of secularism giving shape to historiography, which not only divorced historical study from an explicit transcendent context but also transformed the initially Christian assumptions of much historical study into secular ones and introduced new ones distant from Christian assumptions.[12]

One consequence of these historical trends has been the necessity of distinguishing Christian historiography from other

11. See Herbert Butterfield, *Man on His Past: The Study of the History of Historical Scholarship* (Cambridge, 1969), chapter 2.
12. Important books that discuss some of the themes suggested here in the history of historiography are: Butterfield's *Man on His Past;* James Westfall Thompson, *A History of Historical Writings;* Harry Elmer Barnes, *A History of Historical Writing.* For developments in England, as an illustration, see F. Smith Fussner, *The Historical Revolution: English Historical Writing and Thought, 1580-1640* (New York, 1962); T. P. Peardon, *The Transition in English Historical Writing, 1760-1830* (New York, 1933).

kinds of historiography. In earlier periods the fact that the assumptions of general historical study were Christian was not widely questioned. But certainly by the eighteenth century the perpetuation of Christian assumptions could not be taken for granted. The histories published by, for example, Voltaire on the age of Louis XIV and Edward Gibbon on the decline and fall of the Roman Empire demonstrated that explicitly anti-Christian assumptions might decisively shape the writing of history. The works of the positivist Henry Thomas Buckle on English history, Karl Marx and Friedrich Engels on the bourgeoisie and working classes, and D. F. Strauss on the life of Jesus illustrate the same phenomenon in the nineteenth century. Eminent Christian historians — for example, Lord Acton — nevertheless continued to contribute to the corpus of Christian historiography.[13]

Only gradually and in retrospect have we come to recognize that indeed the great body of modern historiography has developed in one direction while what may be called Christian historiography has gone another direction. This parting of company between Christianity and general historiography was most likely a feature of the nineteenth century. It thus paralleled, or more accurately, it reflected in the area of historical study what Martin Marty has identified as a schism between Christianity and the predominant patterns of Western culture. Christianity increasingly came to be associated primarily with churches while most of the rest of culture came to be regarded as essentially secular and thus unaffected by Christian motives.[14]

In our own century the manifestations of this split between Christianity and general historiography have become much clearer. In the first place, historians in general, with Christians more or less in agreement, have come to treat the category "Christian historiography" either as an impossibility or at best as a sectarianism closer to propaganda than to

13. Two additional works showing points relevant to my theme in the nineteenth century are: G. P. Gooch, *History and Historians in the Nineteenth Century* (Boston, [1913], 1959); Fritz Stern, ed., *The Varieties of History: From Voltaire to the Present* (New York, 1956). Butterfield's *Man on His Past* treats Acton's historiography extensively.
14. Martin Marty, *The Modern Schism: Three Paths to the Secular* (New York, 1969).

scientific or scholarly history. Such was the influence of positivism with its ardent insistence on its own scientific neutrality and lack of metaphysical presuppositions. Many Christians respond to this by referring to themselves not as "Christian historians," but as Christians in their personal beliefs and simply historians like everyone else in their profession. They may, for example, regard their Christianity to mean for their profession, if anything, doing excellently just what the "positivist-liberal" historians do.

There is a second effect of the general split between Christianity and general historiography. Many Christians have not wanted to abandon some relationship between their faith and their profession as historians and so have devoted themselves to the most obvious Christian thing they know — the study of the churches, church history. Beginning with the radical re-examination of the history of the church in the nineteenth century, many eminent church historians have published very competent histories. I mention, for the sake of example, Philip Schaff on general church history, Henry Charles Lea on the medieval Christian era, or Ernst Troeltsch on the social teachings of the Christian church. Many such writers held the respect of secular historians and even fundamentally influenced general historiography. Nevertheless, the result of the concentration on church history has been the adoption of the equation "Christian historiography means church history."

A third effect has been to remove Christian reflection on the nature and meaning of history from the domain of relevance to practicing historians and to relocate it in the "supranatural" domain of theology. Christians, even historians who think about the nature of history, have tended to work in primarily theological categories. On the one hand are the theologies of history that examine the overarching matters of redemptive history, including themes like God's work in history, the meaning of Christ's life and work to history, eschatology, common grace and special grace, providence, divine pattern in history, and so on. On the other side are the explorations of the historicity of the biblical accounts, such as the stories of miracles, the resurrection, the Exodus, the creation. All such work, when competent, can be important to

Christian thinking, but its contribution to working historiography is marginal. Within general historiography such theologies of history are treated as metaphysical or metahistorical or speculative, while contrasted with it is critical history or analytical history.[15] Such distinctions, widely accepted among Christians, make credible the equation "Christian means theology." To be sure, the fact remains that most working historians ignore the whole issue and simply do their history without much awareness of the perspectival character of their work and their methodology.

It is probably correct to say that those historians who translate their Christian commitment in the world into the categories I have identified — personally Christian, professionally excellent, church historian, theologian of history — in practice allow their Christian assumptions a much broader influence upon their historical writing and teaching than we might expect from their theory. For one thing, any Christian who is an historian naturally sympathizes with the legacy of Christian historiography I have already identified. For another, any "excellent" historian or "church historian" will discover numerous crucial conjunctions where his Christian convictions rather easily penetrate his general historical framework, at least in a negative fashion: to resist, for example, notions of history as chance or history as essentially, say, economic-material causation.

There are many eminent exceptions to the trends among historians that I have discussed. I refer to outstanding historians who confess Christ, whose publications are not limited to church history or theology of history, and whose historical writings display evident Christian insight, especially in contrast to the alternative historiographies. I will mention only four historians from the last generation in the English-speaking world. Certain things they share, while in many respects they are very different people.

Carlton J. H. Hayes, a Catholic historian at Columbia University, became the major authority on the history of na-

15. See, e.g., the way Ronald H. Nash works with this dichotomy. The Christian idea of history falls in the first volume: *Ideas of History*, Vol. I: *Speculative Approaches to History;* Vol. II, *The Critical Philosophy of History* (New York, 1969).

tionalism. He originated the idea, by now commonplace, that nationalism in the nineteenth century possessed all the characteristics usually found in religion and was a displacer of the Christian religion in the secular age. His general text on Western civilization, read by a generation of students, and his contribution to the Langer series in modern European history developed the Christian ideas of the multiformity yet integrality of human culture and of the religious character of all ages, including our secular one.[16]

Christopher Dawson, a Catholic who finished his academic career at Harvard University, developed an integrated understanding of a total culture and society unified around essentially religious motives. His insight into the character of Europe, the interweaving of social, economic, political, and ecclesiastical institutions and activities, and the transition from pagan to Christian to secular humanist epochs in Western civilization are indispensable to modern Christian historiography.[17]

R. H. Tawney, an Anglican historian at Oxford University, provided definitive Christian insight into economic history that did not absolutize the economic domain of life as have Marxists, and that understood the role of secular religion-like motives as well as Christian motives in the process of economic development. His *Religion and the Rise of Capitalism* modified the worst features of Max Weber's thesis and formulated a more balanced and reliable assessment of the role of world-view in economic formation and of the manner of economic-historical change.[18]

Herbert Butterfield, a Methodist at Cambridge University, has worked with Christian insight on the era of George

16. See Carter Jefferson, "Carlton J. H. Hayes," in *Historians of Modern Europe: Festschrift for S. William Halperin,* ed. Hans A. Schmitt (Baton Rouge, 1971), pp. 15-35. The article assesses Hayes' work and faith, and the footnotes cite his main histories.

17. Christopher Dawson, *The Dynamics of World History,* ed. John J. Mulloy (New York, 1962), is a good anthology of Dawson's writings. It includes two essays on Dawson by Mulloy and lists his main works up to 1962.

18. A good comment on Tawney's significance and his Christian perspective, which mentions his main works, is D. W. Bebbington, "R. H. Tawney as a Historian," *Christian Graduate* (June 1972), 52-56.

III, on Napoleon, on the history of natural science, on diplomacy, and in many other fields. His awareness, for example, of the grandeur yet sinfulness of men helped him break with the prevailing ideas of the moral progress of history. Perhaps his most crucial gift to historical study has been his pioneering work on the history of historiography, in which he exposes the underlying assumptions that operated within historians' works. I am thinking especially of his works *Man on His Past: The Study of the History of Historical Scholarship* and *The Whig Interpretation of History*.[19]

Many other illustrations of recent Christian historiography and Christian historians could be given. My point is that these four historians wrote their histories with evident Christian insight in our secular age. They did so usually without belabored attention to "what is the Christian view" of this or that, and simply allowed their Christian views of the world and life to shape their work. At the same time they all reflected self-consciously, and in writing, on the importance of Christianity for history and historical reflection.

To summarize. In the last 150 years Christian historiography has entered a new stage. It is no longer the only or the prevailing historiography. In response to the process of secularization and the religious power of secularism, it has commonly taken various forms that often tend to accept some dichotomy between Christianity and general historical study, or which tend to identify Christian historiography with merely church history. Yet in practice many Christian historians have in fact written their histories in such a way that they reveal Christian insight beneficial to ongoing historical study. It is especially on this recent heritage of *de facto* Christian historiography that our generation may build and within which we may find a viable continuing tradition of Christian work in historical study.

19. A good place to start on Butterfield studies is J. H. Elliott and H. G. Koenigsberger, eds., *The Diversity of History: Essays in Honour of Sir Herbert Butterfield* (London, 1970). Included is a complete bibliography of his writings to 1968. It is important to note how many of his works treat the themes of Christianity's relevance to history, diplomacy, international relations, and politics.

Some New Directions for Christian Historiography

The advance of secularization makes new demands on Christian historiography, not the least of which is some measure of self-consciousness about what it ought to be like. Such self-awareness, however, must be unforced and undogmatic. It must not destroy the primary way in which Christian understandings of the world and life ought to shape historical study — that is, it ought simply to come naturally. Christians ought to live their lives and interpret reality in such a way that Christian sensitivities as a matter of course provide the points of reference for their perception of historical events and the historical process.

Yet because the dominant assumptions and values of our age are not Christian, achievement of Christian living and understanding often needs considerable reflection. For this reason systematic Christian philosophical study and societal theory can be important to working historians. I have discovered that the work of the European Christian philosopher Herman Dooyeweerd is exceptionally fertile for historical study. Especially valuable are his theories of the nature of religion, of societal structures, and of the functional modes of existence. He is one of the few Christian thinkers to investigate philosophy of history on a level germane to practicing historians and not simply on the level of metahistory and *Heilsgeschichte*.[20]

As I see it, the ongoing task of Christian historiography is to make functional within the practice of the writing and teaching of history certain primary biblical insights into the nature of human beings, the process of history, cultural work, the interplay of evil and redemption within history, the meaning of justice, stewardship, and love, the nature of the social order, and the structure of created reality. I detect a number

---

20. Dooyeweerd's principal opus is *A New Critique of Theoretical Thought*, 4 vols., trans. David H. Freeman and William S. Young (Amsterdam and Philadelphia, 1953-1957). His own introduction to his work in English is *In the Twilight of Western Thought: Studies in the Pretended Autonomy of Philosophical Thought* (Philadelphia, 1960). Dooyeweerd's festschrift gives details on his bibliography: *Philosophy and Christianity: Philosophical Essays Dedicated to Herman Dooyeweerd* (Kampen, 1965).

of crucial problems that require serious examination during the coming years concerning which a Christian understanding of the world and life can perhaps serve historiography in general. They have to do especially with the "categories" historians use in their enterprise. I will discuss only four of them.

One problem that has not attracted enough scrutiny but troubles historians' work is, "What is the field of investigation of the historian?" The usual answer is "past human activity," or "past culture," or simply "the past." The notion of "the past" rightly refers to the context of historical time — past, present, and future — but it fails to provide an adequate criterion of selection from among all the activities and events that occurred in the past. The past is, after all, immense. What historians usually do in practice is rely heavily on what other historians have already selected and then employ highly personal intuition for the rest.

Involved in the problem is a deepening of insight into the original Christian ideas of historical time, the historical process, and human beings as the makers of history. Fruitful criteria of selection are suggested in Dooyeweerd's works, although I find the way he locates the criteria and his designation of the historical as a limited modal function of reality unhelpful.[21]

We may profitably examine the phenomena that I shall designate "human formative activity" and "historical development." Seen most broadly, history is a fundamental dimension of reality common to people, animals, plants, and material things. They are situated within historical time, understood

21. Dooyeweerd defines the historical as a limited modal aspect of reality. Strictly speaking, he identifies its core meaning as "control" or "mastery" or "power," but he is highly ambiguous about it. He ties these terms to "formative" or "cultural" or "historical." He sometimes uses the terms "cultural formation" or "formative power." However, he also writes of "the opening process," which is transmodal and which depends upon the opening of the historical mode of "control" for it to begin. He has difficulty holding to his own demand that the focus of historical inquiry be modal and tends in his discussion to drift from the narrow notion of "control" to the more total one of "historical development." What follows in my remarks is in disagreement with Dooyeweerd's modal analysis of history and suggests an adaptation of his notion of the opening process. See especially Dooyeweerd, *New Critique*, II, 68-71, 181-365. Also *Twilight*, 62-112.

as past, present, and future in process toward the eschaton. Historians study this process of history from *the special angle of the human activity of the forming of culture which develops the creation*. People *form:* they form things, they form relationships and institutions, they form habits, mores, and rules, they form activities. A variety of other words point to the same phenomenon: they make, they organize, they construct, they produce, they arrange, they institute, they mold, shape, fashion. A series of terms based on the root "to form" indicates the process that is involved in human formative activity: people form things and relationships, they reform them, they transform them, they deform them, they unform them. Then, by means of human formative activity, people may discover and *develop* the possibilities God has established and maintained within the whole of created reality, including people, animals, plants, and material things. The products of this human formative activity, taken as a whole, we may call "culture." When such human activity leads to an unfolding of the creation, we may speak of the fulfillment of creation in historical development. I use the term "develop" not in a narrowly biotic sense of growth, but in its general meaning of "unfold" or "open up." People unfold, open up, develop the creation. They make history out of the developmental possibilities God has structured into created reality. It is central to their divinely given assignment to care for the creation in this way.

The unfolding or development of the creation is a transmodal, dimensional phenomenon that occurs *mutatis mutandis* both in human and in nonhuman realms, as, for example, in the development of the state, of a tornado, or of a plant. The manner in which such development proceeds can be indicated by the terms differentiation, individuation, and reintegration. In so far as the unfolding or development of the creation requires and involves human activity, the process of unfolding becomes the concern of historians, and we may speak of distinctly cultural development entailing uniquely cultural differentiation, individuation, and reintegration. Likewise, formation occurs in both human and nonhuman realms, for example, the formation of a megacorporation, of a glacier, or of a leaf. In so far as the formation is due to human beings, culture is formed in the process of history, and we may refer to cultural formation. It seems to me that the difference between human and nonhuman formation is the human activity of decision-making, which constitutes the crux of what we call authority. Human beings make decisions, thereby exercising authority in responsibility to God and their fellow human beings and the whole creation. So defined, I construe decision-making as no mere intellectual or logical function but an act of the whole person in relationship to other whole persons as well as to animals, plants, and material things.

Viewing history in this way, historians properly so called look for all those human activities in the past in which something — be it a relationship, a habit, a way of life, an art piece, a trend, a movement, a nation, or a church — was formed, reformed, transformed, deformed, unformed, and through which the creation was in some way developed and more fully opened up, or conversely somewhat closed up.

Historians study events, activities, and relationships within the whole cultural context to which they belong. The kinds of formative-developmental activities historians select to investigate depend on the structural context within which they are looking. An historian of American politics looks principally at politically formative and developmental acts, events, and institutions set within American culture and society. An historian of nineteenth-century working-class housing in Toronto studies those acts, designs, and trends that are formative and developmental for such urban domestic living in Canada. An historian of French gardening examines the human act of cultivating and arranging flowers and trees in their social, political, economic, and horticultural setting. And so on. The special context may be large or small, this or that, here or there, since everything people devote themselves to in the development of culture is potentially of interest to historians. We may speak of those human acts that are formative-developmental in a certain context as influential, hence as historical acts. Those that are especially influential, exceptionally formative and developmental, are the acts that historians may call historically significant.

I have perhaps said enough to indicate what I find to be a worthwhile line of exploration.

A second problem Christian historians may beneficially study is the role of "religion" in the making of culture, especially now that our culture is secular. The usual thing is to regard religion as an aspect of culture, which is identified with churches, worship, and little else. In this view religion may or may not be important to a culture, depending on the situation. It is usual to speak of the medieval *Corpus Christianum*, where the Christian church was central, as religious, but, for example, to regard twentieth-century America or the Soviet Union as not very religious. The category "religion" is treated as something that may be "lost" or as something a person can "get." It is not considered an abiding feature of human life in all times and cultures. At the same time, however, historians will talk of "ideas" and "ideologies" that appear to have such a motivating hold upon human affairs that curiously they seem to possess the characteristics normally ascribed to religious belief.

A view that seems to give a better account of the matters this problem raises as faced by historians in the modern era is, as Martin Marty puts it, "that secularization did *not* mean the disappearance of religion so much as its relocation."[22] A special contribution of Christian historians like Carlton J. H. Hayes and Christopher Dawson is their recognition that religion is a permanent and defining characteristic of human culture, which, after the passing of the Christian centuries, emerges in different secular manifestations. Dooyeweerd works with the idea of "religious ground motives," which underlie and inwardly shape a civilization. In our own era the religious ground motive can perhaps be described broadly as secularist and humanist, superseding the Christian motive of the medieval period and the pagan one of the Greek-Roman epoch.

I find that the category "religious motive" provides essential foundational insight into any civilization — Islamic, Hindu, Buddhist, Christian, secular humanist — for therein lies a civilization's central defining characteristic. Every aspect of a civilization — cultic, political, economic, familial, artistic, scientific — is unmistakably shaped by it. In this view the terms "Christian" and "secular" are both taken to be religious terms.

22. Marty, p. 11.

They both refer to the identifiably religious motives known to invest a civilization or a society with distinctive character displayed in the operative norms and values as well as in the actual patterns of institutionalization and ordinary practice within the civilization or society.

In our secular Western civilization I find it necessary to further specify the particular ways in which the central religious motive is directed to the formation and development of culture. Provisionally, the category of "socio-cultural motive" or "cultural ideal" helps me identify the many movements that compete in the formation of various societies in Western civilization. For example, in the 1850s and 1860s in Italy, during the years of the *Risorgimento*, I find these principal socio-cultural motives among others to be operative, each with local variants: the Catholic ultramontanism of the papacy of Pius IX; the absolutist aristocratic monarchism of an *ancien régime* style in Naples; a liberal aristocratic monarchism tied to Piedmont, Count Cavour's leadership, and new industrial capitalism; a radical democratism of a Mazzinian variety. Each of these socio-cultural motives channels a Catholic Christian or secular religious motive into the cultural formation of society in a total way. Each has its own principle of authority, its own principle of socio-cultural organization, its own core peoplehood, its own version of "the enemy," its own typical modes of institutionalization, and other characteristics. Each is not merely an intellectual concept worked out by philosophers or great leaders, but is a motivating spirit that drives and unifies the historically formative activity of a distinctive cultural movement of people. The characteristics of a socio-cultural motive are detectable not only in written and spoken explanations, but also in the actions of people and in the function and structure of their institutions and societal relationships. I can only suggest here a sort of category that I believe merits extensive examination in the actual historical situation.

A third important matter for the future of Christian historiography and other historiographies as well is the question of historical judgments. All varieties of historiography make judgments of many kinds that are disclosed in the body of published histories, even though some historians, in the interests of a positivist idea of objectivity, deny that this is so. The problem is not whether or not to make judgments but what judgments to make and what norms to use in making them. The question needs serious study, for it is here that the historian's assumptions and perspective are so explicitly detectable. Judgments made by an historian appear especially in the adjectives and adverbs used, in the reasons and explanations he gives for some event, in the description of what was or was not part of the scene, in the recognition of interrelationships, and in many other ways. Historical judgment is implicit within, and not separable from, the act of determining historical factuality.

Let me illustrate from a few pages in *The Age of the Democratic Revolution,* Volume 1, by R. R. Palmer of Yale University. I have chosen this book and passage at random from a shelf of historical monographs in my library. In a section on the aristocracy in the late eighteenth century, Palmer makes these various kinds of judgments: The English House of Commons was "far more broadly based" than the French Parlement of Dauphiny; William Pitt at age 24 was "a man of great talents and understanding in certain fields"; studies at Oxford were "no more difficult, and no more enlightening" than those at Grenoble; France was "a rich country with a chronically impoverished government"; in France class consciousness "heightened"; the French aristocratic social system created "evils" that needed remedy.[23] Palmer's judgments assume his allegiance to certain norms, which he believes would best regulate the functioning of the institutions and people he studies. In these illustrations his judgments pertain to political, intellectual, moral, educational, economic, and social norms. I am not arguing that Palmer should not have made these judgments, that his norms are right or wrong, or his judgments good or bad ones. I simply observe that he, along with all historians, made them and that they assume a constellation of norms covering a wide range of human affairs as well as sufficient understanding and insight into the affairs he studies to allow the making of judgments about how well the institutions or people function in relation to those norms.

23. Princeton, 1969, pp. 77-79.

The contribution of Christian values and insights to this problem of historical judgments can be significant. The central kind of judgments historians must make involves whether or not an event, a movement, someone, an activity is historically significant. Then he must make judgments relating to the kind of structural category he investigates. If it has to do with, say, the English parliament, then political-historical judgments are necessary in which the historian must possess detailed special knowledge of political institutions, adequate understanding of politics, and even some political theory. This he must arrange in some way according to the norm of justice or injustice and its concrete special variants. For instance, the judgment that the English House of Commons was "far more broadly based" implies the presence within Palmer's normative horizon of some norm concerning how the parliament should be based in order for justice to be practiced in that era. Specifically, the "far more broadly based" English parliament is, according to that norm, better than the French Parlement of Dauphiny. Similar remarks may be made about norms appropriate to industry and commerce in economic history, norms relevant to family history or social class history, or the history of art.

As my comments should indicate, the question of historical judgments is vast. Nevertheless it remains largely unexplored by historians, except perhaps as a function of merely linguistic-logical analysis. The relationship between the actual happenings and an historian's presuppositions, his values, his identification of norms, his judgment with respect to the norms needs scrutiny. Likewise, the problem of forming judgments and specifying norms in periods and cultures different from our own must be studied.

A fourth line of work I shall only mention. Christian historians, in the light of their special insights into the world and life, need to engage in extensive historical revision, reworking the framework within which we view the history of Western civilization and other civilizations. The revision of many currently accepted historical accounts follows. Competent Christian historiography today has before it the work of reexamining the process of history and perhaps offering through its reinterpretation of history some new insights, new formulations of old problems, improved descriptions of why and how things developed as they did. To this end the study of the history of historiography is indispensable to understanding why historians have seen and interpreted history as they have. Herbert Butterfield's works demonstrate this. The task of revision is potentially very rewarding.

These four questions may suffice to indicate some new directions for Christian historiography today based on the legacy of earlier Christian historians, and in interaction with other contemporary historiographies. Much more could be said.

A Closing Remark

The gist of my argument has been this. Historians who are Christians have a responsibility to carry on their study of history in such a way that their written and taught histories may be shaped by the insights into the nature of history, created reality, human beings, societal structures, evil and redemption, and the healthful norms that a Christian world-and-life-view provides. Christian historical study, when competently pursued, can suggest fruitful ways of viewing the historical process and of revising the accepted accounts of that process. It may thereby serve historians of other perspectives while it promotes the development of historical understanding in our times. Christian historical study today may draw upon an ancient tradition that is still very much alive and whose legacy has fundamentally influenced general historiography. With a measure of self-consciousness about the philosophical and methodological issues of historical study, Christian historians may better go about their work in our secular age amid the multitude of rival and conflicting historical interpretations. Some crucial areas of exploration await their work.

In the final analysis, the merits of Christian historiography will depend on the liberation it helps provide for our historical understanding. It is possible that competent and sensible work in historical study may indeed contribute to what Collingwood called "a reorientation of the entire structure of human thought." This is a task our secular age urgently requires.

The Muse Meets the Master: Clio and Christ

DONALD A. MACPHEE

HISTORY, it seems to me, is uniquely positioned among the liberal arts and sciences to serve as an example of faith/learning relationships. The Christian revelation, after all, is firmly planted in space and *time*, and to study these relationships is to involve the historian with the really crucial issues of his discipline.

The question of relating history (or any other discipline) to one's faith can be discussed on at least two levels. First, in a philosophical, theoretical, or conceptual sense: Can the historian who is also a Christian pursue his craft and hold his beliefs with intellectual honesty and integrity? What is the larger meaning of his discipline and how can it be reconciled with his value and belief system? Most historians, especially American historians, have paid relatively little attention to these aspects of their work. And secondly, what are the practical implications of my faith for my life and work as a practicing historian? How does it affect my teaching and my writing? Is the affirmation of my faith as a professional explicit, implicit, or both? In other words, how are history and Christianity related in theory and practice, by precept and example, in my role as scholar and as teacher? In commenting on these two dimensions of the question, I will be making a kind of interim report on one working historian's attempt to understand the links of his craft with his faith. There is lively debate going on among historians, social scientists, philosophers, and theologians on many of these points and it would be arrogant and foolish for me to claim any special insight on such matters.[1]

1. The literature on the relation of the Christian faith to history is extensive and growing; see, for instance, M. Howard Rienstra, "Christianity and History: a Bibliographical Essay" in this volume.

The philosophical issues and tensions in historical learning and the Christian faith must, I believe, be put in the context of the peculiarly hybrid and integrative nature of history as a discipline. Contemporary American historians may be thought of as scattered along a kind of disciplinary continuum. Toward one end of the continuum are those historians who regard their discipline as essentially a social science and attempt to become most rigorously "behavorial" and "scientific." They study individual social phenomena as members of a class of phenomena, expecting them to yield generalizations that can be demonstrated with a high degree of predictive value.[2] Toward the other end of the continuum are historians who identify more closely with the humanistic disciplines. Their work is more subjective and intuitive, more preoccupied with specific human experiences, in an effort to deal with the philosophical, religious, ethical, and aesthetic dimensions of the past.

In practice, however, it is my observation that most historians correctly recognize that their discipline embraces elements of both the social sciences and the humanities, and that identification with one or the other is largely a matter of administrative convenience and risks distortion of the essential catholicity of their field. In pursuing his task the historian attempts to integrate into his work the insights and solidly demonstrated generalizations offered by the social sciences; but he is also interested in unique events and individuals. He is as rigorous as possible in gathering and analyzing his data; but he recognizes that the study and writing of history also involves important elements of imagination and creativity.

Indeed, as a group of my colleagues has recently suggested, "values are deeply imbedded in the historian's very methodology. Since he is compelled to select from the infinitely diverse data of human experience the 'significant' and the 'meaningful,' the historian defines the area of his investigation and the questions he asks of his data in terms of his value assumptions or presuppositions." Accordingly, historical

2. Edward N. Saveth, ed., *American History and the Social Sciences* (New York, 1964), explores the possibilities and limitations of this relationship.

"truth," to the extent finite historians are able to determine it, is always contingent; and historians tend to retain a degree of intellectual modesty and tentativeness about their understanding of the past.[3]

By 1950, when I was beginning my graduate study, these issues had been confronted by some of the most distinguished of American historians, leading them to a searching examination of the very nature of the historical enterprise. Illustrative of the scholarly exchanges that resulted were the presidential addresses to the American Historical Association of two of the giants of the profession (Charles A. Beard in 1934 and Samuel E. Morison in 1950), significantly entitled "Written History as an Act of Faith" and "Faith of a Historian."[4] Both Beard and Morison displayed the typically American pragmatic approach to their task in constructing their positions from whatever source seemed meaningful, without excessive concern for inconsistency or paradox. Beard, for example, rejected the possibility of history as a pure science, but also attacked extreme relativism. He called for historians to pay attention to and use the work of the related social science disciplines, even those professing to be "value-free," and yet insisted that the historian commit himself to a particular vision of the future (for Beard a "collectivist democracy"). His own work showed clearly the effects of his frame of reference on his scholarship.

Morison, an historian of great breadth and literary style, attacked — and to some extent caricatured — Beard's relativism. He argued convincingly for a common sense notion of objectivity, and emphasized such qualities as honesty, skepticism, balance, and a philosophy of life. Although on the spectrum described above, Morison falls closer to the humanities pole and Beard to the social sciences, it is clear that any such categorization hardly does justice to the subtleties and pragmatism of their respective approaches.

The early nineteen-sixties brought new and less doctrinaire definitions of "scientific" history than had been ad-

3. In this section, I have drawn on some unpublished materials developed in California by the History Advisory Panel of a Social Sciences Study Committee.
4. *American Historical Review,* XXXIX, 219-229; LVI, 261-275.

vanced in the previous century: political and economic historians drew on quantitative techniques and learned the strange new language of the computer (some even enjoyed being called "cliometricians");[5] social historians increasingly used concepts of class and status developed by sociology; and others ventured into the murky waters of personality theory.[6] The later sixties saw a passionate return among so-called radical historians to attempts to press the past into the service of the present, or, in some cases, to become so engrossed in problems of the present as to reject the past entirely. These historians, mostly from the New Left, raised fundamental questions about areas of the American past earlier commanding a broad consensus among scholars.[7]

These views and many others, ancient and modern, have contributed to the intellectual milieu in which I have been trained and have worked. At the same time, my personal life-commitment since before graduate school days has been to the Christian faith. While this commitment has captured and engrossed my mind — my reason, if you will — it has also transcended my reason. For its central act was an act of faith— faith in Jesus Christ as Savior and Lord. This has given me a set of presuppositions, a prior commitment to a source of ultimate truth and reality.

The question then remains: what has Clio to do with Christ? While I confess that I have not been absorbed over the years in a self-conscious effort to integrate or reconcile my Christian faith and my daily historical forays, if I were to set down some elements of the "faith of this historian," they would look something like the following:

1. *History is a meaningful story, characterized and perhaps best represented graphically by linear direction rather than*

5. A very helpful collection of essays is found in Robert P. Swierenga, ed., *Quantification in American History: Theory and Research* (New York, 1970).
6. See, e.g., Stanley Elkins' controversial treatment "Slavery and Personality," *Slavery* (New York, 1959), pp. 81-139.
7. A good sampling of this point of view is brought together in Barton J. Bernstein, ed., *Towards a New Past: Dissenting Essays in American History* (New York, 1969).

by repetitive cycles or a spiral of progress.[8] This understanding of history, as Professor Montgomery has suggested, involves God's mighty act as Creator (in the beginning); as Redeemer (at the center or focal point, as God intervened in history in the person of his Son); and as Sanctifier (in climax with the final judgment).[9] Its authority rests on the biblical revelation, and it draws on the insights of later writers like Augustine and the Reformers.

2. *There is an objective reality to past events.* The subject-object controversy as it relates to historical reality is long and complex, and I suggest that those Christian apologists who have attempted to interpret the views of the leading contenders have tended to polarize unfairly those with differing but not necessarily irreconcilable positions. Be that as it may, my Christian bias tends at this point to reinforce what I think most of my colleagues in history believe anyway — that history really did happen. Thus, the emphases of philosopher-historians like Dilthey, Croce, Ortega y Gasset, Collingwood, and others on history as primarily a philosophical enterprise, as the "object being absorbed by the subject,"[10] involving essentially the "reenactment of past thoughts in the historian's own mind,"[11] although of value in reminding us of the subjective element in history and of differences in approach between the natural sciences and history,[12] seem at least potentially contrary both to the validity of the Christian revelation and to observed reality, and they hold the seeds of a kind of solipsism.

Page Smith has noted the practical importance of this point in observing that the "dimension of the historic alone prevents us from being crushed by the weight of the present; it is equally important to hold fast to the objective nature of the historic as a bulwark against the encroachment of the

8. This paradigm has been fully developed by Earle E. Cairns, "Philosophy of History," in *Contemporary Evangelical Thought,* ed. Carl F. H. Henry (New York, 1957).

9. John Warwick Montgomery, "Where is History Going?" *His,* May, 1971, p. 11.

10. Page Smith, *The Historian and History* (New York, 1964), p. 239.

11. R. G. Collingwood, *The Idea of History* (Oxford, 1946), p. 215.

12. W. H. Walsh, *Philosophy of History* (New York, 1960), p. 56.

subjective. . . . It is the objective nature of our historic life which offers the means for drawing modern man out of his increasingly sterile subjectivism and back into an inhabitable, if grossly imperfect, world."[13] (Note that I am referring to "objective" here in the sense of the reality of verifiable facts— their historicity — and not "objectivity" as a realizable goal of the historian. We'll get to that later.)

3. *Although there is an objective reality to the past, all human attempts at reconstruction are necessarily imperfect, partial, and therefore distorted images of that reality.* This point, of course, is crucial and has special relevance to a Christian understanding of man and history. Sydney E. Mead has said: History is "knowable and known in part by man but known completely and ultimately only to God. . . . The assertion that only God knows the final end of the story means that all human constructions of segments of it are limited and tentative. . . . This in turn means that men must live by faith in the God of the living — that is, the God of those living in history."[14]

Mead also makes the point that to the Christian the paths of both his intellectual and religious quests lead ultimately to the same point: ". . . the God preeminently revealed in Jesus Christ, the author of his faith *and* the Lord of all his history. . . . His [the Christian's] assertion in faith is a declaration of the primary presupposition of his intellectual quest" (p. 92). The first letter to the Corinthian church perhaps says it best: "Now my knowledge is imperfect, but then I shall know as fully as God knows me" (I Cor. 13:12).

There are, of course, other aspects to this contingency and incompleteness of the historical record that are commonplace to the working historian, Christian and non-Christian alike. They have to do with such matters as fortuity or chance in the availability of sources (the chemist can simply order experimental materials from the supply room, while the historian must work with what comes to hand); distortion in the sources available (history tends to favor those who keep records,

13. Smith, pp. 239-240.
14. Sydney E. Mead, "Church History Explained," *New Theology*, Vol. 1, eds. Marty and Peerman (New York, 1964), p. 92.

usually the powerful and the affluent, and to exaggerate the dramatic, bizarre, and catastrophic); the danger of the *fait accompli* (since we know how "things came out," we have difficulty understanding history on its own terms); the *post hoc propter hoc* fallacy (because something happened *after* something else, we are tempted to conclude that it happened *because* of it); the paradox of too few and too many facts (we know too little of the remote past and of the third world, while our computers are choking on the data of the modern Western world).

4. *Because the historian is neither able nor interested in reproducing the past in toto — undifferentiated and without interpretation — central to his task is the process of selection of material and the assigning of pattern and meaning to that material.* This process raises several important questions for the historian, particularly for the Christian historian. Let me comment very selectively on three interrelated aspects: the historian's "frame of reference," the question of "objectivity," and the role of "moral judgment" in history.

The notion of the "frame of reference" of the historian is hardly controvertible in its most obvious sense. Very few historians today would contend that the historical record carries its own interpretation, or that the historian can or should divest himself of any presuppositions in approaching his sources.[15] A statement in Bulletin No. 54 of the Social Science Research Council, called "Theory and Practice in Historical Study," describes the reality of writing history: ". . . every written history . . . is a selection of facts made by some person . . . and is ordered or organized under the influence of a scheme of reference, interest, or emphasis . . . in the thought of the author. . . ."[16]

The frame of reference, point of view, value system, bias — whatever designation it is given — must, of course, be balanced with liberal quantities of "judicious skepticism," intellectual honesty, and humility, as we shall suggest shortly, but

15. John Warwick Montgomery's views on this subject have stimulated a lively debate in the journals: see the several exchanges cited in Rienstra's bibliography, p. 188.
16. New York, 1946, p. 135.

the exercise of this very intellectual honesty requires a recognition by the historian of his commitment; historical explanation itself demands some principle of selection.

Sydney Mead, speaking to the particular pattern of commitments held by the Christian historian, presses this point to its conclusion:

> . . . every written history is at least implicitly an explanation and defense of the allegiance — the faith — of the historian. It points to that to which the historian is committed. In this respect the Christian historian does not differ from the non-Christian historians. His conflict with them, if any, is a conflict of allegiances — of faiths — and should be recognized as such. This means that the basic differences between historians — or between schools of historians — are theological and/or philosophical, and cannot be resolved by historical methods. This suggests at least that theology *is* 'the Queen of the sciences,' the final arbiter between the claims of the disciplines and between the schools within disciplines.[17]

Or, as Alan Richardson put it: "The historian's final judgment of the evidence will, then, in the last resort, and after as rigorous a critical appraisal as he can make, be determined by *the kind of man he is.*"[18]

In many ways the notion of objectivity as it applies to the work of the historian lacks substance and meaning; but, as one historian said, "its ghost lingers on, crying out to be exorcised and laid to rest once for all."[19] Objectivity as the scholarly ideal of the nineteenth-century "scientific" historian was dealt severe blows by both relativism and historicism at the end of the century, but continuing attempts were made to cling to the ideal. Page Smith suggests that "instead of debating the degree of objectivity that the historian might hope to attain, it would be far better to conceive of the task of the historian as one of sympathetic understanding of his subject, a matter of attachment rather than detachment, of love rather than aloofness" (p. 155).

Considered in this sense, history becomes more a moral than a scientific undertaking. "Subjective" in this context

17. Mead, p. 83.
18. *History, Sacred and Profane* (London, 1964), p. 203.
19. Smith, p. 154.

refers to the condition in which the historian as a living human being "grasps the past through a kind of extension of his sensory apparatus, with the help of his critical faculties." To say the historian is objective is to suggest that he is "somehow outside of time, outside of the flux of human events, and thus views man with cold, Olympian detachment" (p. 156). Detachment of this sort (rather than the coincidental detachment of being removed in time from the events he is describing) can become a kind of denial of the reality of the human condition itself in a vain attempt at achieving what we have described earlier as that perfect knowledge known only to God.

And the historian — whether Christian or not — if he is true to his calling, is involved in the making of moral judgments. Since the actions of individuals and groups make up the stuff of history, and since these actions have involved values and ideals, the historian cannot and should not avoid taking a position on issues confronting him. For the interpreter of twentieth-century Europe, Nazi Germany is an obvious example; for the American historian, the Civil War and Negro slavery pose the classic case.

"Revisionist" historians of the 1940's, like James G. Randall and Avery Craven, giving lip service to the ideal of a "scientific, neutral, value-free" conception of history, rejected the stern judgments on slavery made by men like von Holst and Rhodes in the post-Civil War period, and blamed only emotionalism on both sides, caused by overheated abolitionists and a "blundering generation" of politicians who should have and could have compromised issues dividing the North and South.

Arthur Schlesinger, Jr., with the trauma of World War II still fresh in his consciousness in 1949, provided the most insightful critique of the revisionist position.[20] Chiding his fellow historians for being so easily deluded, Schlesinger argued that although the historian should not "roam through the past ladling out individual praise and blame . . . there are certain

20. Arthur M. Schlesinger, Jr., "The Causes of the Civil War: A Note on Historical Sentimentalism," *The Partisan Review*, XVI (1949), 969-981.

essential issues on which it is necessary for the historian to have a position if he is to understand the great conflicts of history." Clearly, involuntary servitude was one of these. It is interesting to note that Schlesinger had been deeply affected by the insights of the "theologians of crisis," especially Reinhold Niebuhr. His reference to the revisionist position as "a touching afterglow of the admirable nineteenth century faith in the full rationality and perfectibility of man" and his confession that "we gravely overrated man's capacity to solve the problems of existence within the terms of history," are consistent with the neo-orthodox critique of liberal optimism.

But Schlesinger's analysis saw only the proximate solution — the periodic necessity for the breaking of the logjam men create for themselves by violent outbursts like the Civil War (or World War II). Schlesinger was right, as far as he went, in describing history as "not a redeemer, promising to solve all human problems in time; nor . . . man capable of transcending the limitations of his being." What he missed, of course, was that although *history* is not a redeemer, a redeemer nevertheless is there, and that man can transcend his dilemma through faith in this savior-redeemer.

If the historian is to display sympathetic understanding for, rather than detachment from, his subject, and is to make moral judgments on the great issues he confronts, something must be said about the qualities that prevent his work from becoming a mere panegyric or heavy-handed boorishness. I would suggest that the qualities to be cultivated and cherished most by the historian are intellectual honesty in searching for the truth about the past; intellectual humility regarding the limits of human insight and understanding; judiciousness in making assessments; a healthy skepticism of sources; painstaking workmanship; a compassionate spirit; and a sense of balance and proportion (Morison uses the French word *mesure* here). It is to these qualities of mind and heart that we must look rather than to a scientific methodology as the most promising for the historical enterprise.

Finally, what difference does any of this make to the encounter I have with a class in nineteenth-century America at 8:00 on M W F ? We have been discussing primarily the conceptualization of a discipline as it relates to the Christian faith. How is this view, if at all valid, to affect my teaching? Let me say first that my own teaching has all been on state-supported campuses, and although the philosophical foundation is presumably identical, the applications will no doubt vary on secular and Christian campuses. My observations on this more practical side of our topic are all, in a sense, merely variations on the same theme and may be stating the obvious:

1. If the Christian revelation is to be related to our discipline in a substantive and meaningful way, attempts at integration should confront the central issues, the important questions, and not involve only secondary or tangential problems. In discussing the American Revolution, for example, one might consider Alan Heimert's recent thesis concerning the social and political views of evangelicals and their links with the Great Awakening,[21] or Timothy Smith's revision of our understanding of the relation of revivalists and social reform in the antebellum period.[22] To illustrate by exaggeration, this approach would seem more instructive than commenting on instances of prayer in the continental congresses as evidence of Christian influence in history. It should involve the entire way we look at a problem, perhaps more in the manner of Jacques Ellul in the social sciences or H. R. Rookmaaker in the arts.[23]

2. I also think that some of the most effective attempts at an integration are perhaps not really attempts at all, but are intuitive and unplanned moments of shared insight between instructor and student. If our Christian presuppositions are at peace rather than at war with our conception of our role as

21. *Religion and the American Mind from the Great Awakening to the Revolution* (Cambridge, Mass., 1966). See also a review-article by M. Howard Matteson-Boze in *Fides et Historia*, IV, 1 (Fall 1971), 4-16.
22. *Revivalism and Social Reform* (New York, 1957).
23. Useful commentaries on Ellul's contributions are found in James Y. Holloway, ed., *Introducing Jacques Ellul* (Grand Rapids, Michigan, 1970), and Russell Heddendorf, "The Christian World of Jacques Ellul," *The Christian Scholar's Review*, II, 4 (1973), 291-307. Professor Rookmaaker's *Modern Art and the Death of a Culture* (London, 1970) is a serious attempt, from a Reformed perspective, to interpret the impact on Western society of changes in the visual arts (primarily painting) since the Renaissance.

scholar-teacher, then applications will come in a natural way—
not forced, mechanical, or tacked on for effect, or out of pious
compulsion.

3. For myself, rather than thinking in terms of integration (which implies a prior separation), I would rather think
in terms of simply leaving in the Christian options, or to put
it another way, trying to tell a balanced and complete story.
I assume no arbitrary or artificial separation between religious
and historical study. Man's religious experience is an essential
part of his story. To leave it out is reductionism as much as is
economic determinism; to treat it unfairly or superficially is
bad history, just as is indoctrination or special pleading. Evangelical Christianity *was* crucial to the nineteenth-century
American religious and social experience; moral issues *were*
significant in the sectional conflict; the religious motivation
was significant to the reform movements of the 1830s and
1840s.

4. We should also be aware of the availability to us as
teacher-scholars of both explicit and implicit affirmations of
our faith. I put aside here an exploration of the personal,
caring, helping relationships with students and colleagues
that add a rich dimension of humanness, warmth, and love
to the academic community. This kind of integration of one's
professional and personal life, however, is as exciting to me
as the present topic. I refer rather to the whole range of
possibilities, from stating explicitly at the beginning of a
course that "these are my biases," to simply being guided
in one's treatment of a subject by the implications of a Christian world-view. These alternatives, of course, are not mutually exclusive, and in regard to the earlier principle of natural-
ness, we will vary in approach depending on our personality,
style, convictions, and the setting in which we find ourselves.

At the very least, though, it seems to me that the Christian
historian will take seriously the implications of his faith in
his appraisal of man and society and will recognize as well
its potential as a unifying principle in the face of the frag-
mentation of modern knowledge. St. Paul, speaking of Christ,
provides us with the starting point for our quest: "In him all
things were created in heaven and on earth, visible and in-

visible, whether thrones or dominions or principalities or authorities — all things were created through him and for him. He is before all things, and in him all things hold together" (Col. 1:16-17).

History as a Social Science: A Christian's Response

EDWIN J. VAN KLEY

IS HISTORY an art or a science? The argument is almost as old as written history itself. On the one hand, so much of the historian's effort goes into the reconstruction of past events or epochs — much of it imaginative reconstruction to bridge the gaps between his inadequate sources — that he often sees his craft more akin to art than to science. On the other hand, all historians agree that the gathering and evaluating of evidence should proceed as scientifically as possible, and even those most dedicated to the simple re-creation of past events make all sorts of generalizations, consciously and otherwise, and are thus open to the preachment that they should make scientifically verifiable generalizations.

But the issue runs deeper than a mere quarrel between two groups of historians, one of which thinks it makes more responsible generalizations than the other. It also touches the purpose and object of the historian's inquiry. Traditional historians — perhaps most historians — have usually seen their task as almost the reverse of the scientist's. While the scientist or social scientist gathers particular bits of information to formulate and test a generalization, the traditional historian has focused on the particulars themselves. The illumination of the particular event, epoch, or person has been his goal, rather than any generalization embracing and explaining it and other particulars. Most historians almost instinctively realize that to subsume the particular event or person under a general category or law dehumanizes it, strips it of its uniqueness and richness, and thus distorts the truth about it. Perhaps that is why most historians are much better at breaking than making generalizations. In fact, they commonly use generalizations to lead them to the particulars rather than the other way around. They treat generalizations like scaffolding, useful to help understand the particulars but dispensable once that goal is achieved.

Again, the purpose of this enterprise is as old as the writing of history. Herodotus said he wrote "in order that what men have done may not be forgotten through the passage of time, and so that the great and admirable deeds performed both by Greeks and by barbarians may not be without honor." But why should we remember what men have done? Because, I suppose, we are men and because we are shaped by what our ancestors have done, and thus to know what they have done is an essential part of self-knowledge. How can Americans understand themselves without knowing a great deal about the republic's history and its European antecedents? How can Christians understand themselves without knowing what God's people have believed and done and how they have interacted with other human communities in the past? How can any humans understand themselves without knowing something about the varied experiences of the human community on the globe? How can Christians preach and implement God's revelation without knowing, in an historical sense, both themselves and other human communities? To answer questions like these, traditional historians — Christian and humanist — have assumed the task of preserving and interpreting the past of mankind for its present members.

In keeping with this traditional concept of their task, historians have usually insisted that history be written in ordinary language, not for fellow historians but for the general educated public. They do not want historians to describe the process of their research (how they found and evaluated the sources); they want a readable description of the results of that research, a reconstruction of what happened. The ability to tell the stories accurately and artistically has never been despised by professional historians. They have stressed the virtues of good writing to a far greater degree than have social scientists, for example. While it is true that much historical literature is read only by other historians, a great many historians do indeed write for a larger public.

Historians have usually regarded teaching in the same way. They assume that their courses are for all students, not just for those who intend to specialize in the discipline. They do not usually begin, as courses in the social sciences do, with basic principles and definitions of terms to be mastered before one can be introduced to the discipline. There is no specialized jargon necessary to understand them. Now this traditional view of the historian's task is once again being seriously challenged by the recent trend among some historians to view their profession as one of the social sciences and to accept the methods and assumptions of the social sciences.

For example, an increasingly large number of books and articles currently being published falls into the category of social history. In one fashion or another they deal with the history of the masses, of ordinary people and their institutions, social organizations, economic endeavors and accomplishments. The history of the family is enjoying considerable interest. The growing importance of social history does not merely indicate that historians have found new subjects for investigation; it has profound methodological and philosophical implications as well. If, for example, an historian decides to study peasant families in eighteenth-century Austria instead of the ruling Hapsburg family, he is confronted with totally different sorts of source material. Peasant families left no letters to friends or memoirs that were subsequently preserved in family libraries. It is probably impossible to write the history of a single peasant family. Consequently, our historian must collect statistics; he wants to know how many peasants owned land, how many people lived in a typical peasant's house, at what age most peasants married, how many children they typically had, what percentage of them were baptized, what the inheritance laws and customs were, how landless peasants supported themselves, what price they received for the products they raised, what taxes and rents they paid, and the like. To do this sort of research the historian must develop reliable ways of handling statistics. In fact, of course, economists, sociologists, and political scientists have already done that. But our historian must now learn how to use these statistical methods. He begins to read and study as much economics and sociology as history. Perhaps he even studies computer programming.

Involvement in the new methods also tends to foster the assumption that scientifically verifiable generalizations are the most important products of historical research. Statistics are usually compiled to support generalizations. An economist or a sociologist, for example, collects unemployment statistics in the black and white neighborhoods of Chicago in order to support or refute the generalization that unemployment is higher among blacks than among whites. To return to our Austrian peasant families, the historian may collect statistics to show that the so-called modern nuclear family antedates the industrial revolution and is not, as formerly believed, one of its consequences.[1] The researcher has moved away from the illumination of the particular as his major task to the formulation of generalizations about large groups of people. He has, in short, become more scientific. He may also find that his generalization about Austrian peasant families becomes still more interesting to him if he compares them with Indian or Chinese peasant families.[2] Now he is involved in comparative history.

We could follow the example much further, but perhaps most of the important consequences of such social history are already apparent: it involves the historical use of methods borrowed from the social sciences, thereby breaking down or at least reducing the distinctions between these disciplines. It makes the social historian much more scientific than the traditional historian in that he is actually collecting raw statistical data in search of a scientific generalization. The complexity of the tools and procedures for such research forces its practitioners to pay much more attention to techniques and methods than traditional historians usually do. Both the nonpolitical subject and the desirability of cross-cultural comparisons tend to reduce the importance of national history or the history of single civilizations. Finally, such a social historian may find it difficult to think of his task as the preser-

1. This generalization is in fact made in the article I have been using as an example: Lutz K. Berkner, "The Stem Family and the Development Cycle of the Peasant Household: An Eighteenth-Century Austrian Example," *American Historical Review*, LXXVII, 2 (April 1972), 398-418.
2. Professor Berkner does not make these comparisons.

vation of the past for the edification of his fellow citizens in anything like the traditional sense, and he probably will write up his findings for fellow experts rather than for the general educated public. This last consideration has predictable effects on his literary style. While such consequences do not inevitably result from using the new techniques, they certainly seem to be the prevailing tendencies.

Even more recent and more faddish has been the new interest in psychological techniques for historical research. Its enthusiasts contend that since biography has always been important to historians, they should try to use the insights of psychologists and psychoanalysts to help understand historical personalities. Human behavior and motivation are very complex, they say, and the biographer who merely illumines the surface or public life of a man like Napoleon, Bismarck, or Hitler has not served his readers very well. He should also search for symptoms of known personality types or identifiable psychological problems to help us really understand the great men of history. In fact, some psycho-historians have observed that all biographers make psychological judgments and inferences about their subjects, but that they usually do so without first getting the psychology straight. Historians should, they contend, make conscious rather than unconscious psychological judgments, and they should become knowledgeable about current psychological theory before they make any at all.

Thus, psycho-history also tends to blur the distinction between historians and social scientists — in this case between historians and psychologists. On the surface, unlike social history, it seems to focus attention on the particular rather than on the scientific generalization. In practice, however, it tends to categorize the individual subject once the researcher has found evidence for a known personality type or an identifiable psychological malady. The individual then becomes another instance of the general type — a manic-depressive, for instance. Perhaps the most dangerous thing about psycho-history is the tendency to start with the generalization — with the personality type or psychological aberration — and to assume the presence in the subject of all the charac-

teristics of such a general type once some of those characteristics have been found. It is difficult enough to psychoanalyze
a living person; it often requires hundreds of probing sessions
extended over long periods of time, sometimes years. For
historical subjects the detailed evidence necessary for an
accurate diagnosis simply does not exist. Consequently, the
psycho-historian is forced to make his diagnosis on insufficient
evidence and to assume the rest of the symptoms. Such a
diagnosis may easily be wrong. Furthermore, to assume the
existence of the remaining symptoms not only encourages the
researcher to say things about his subject that cannot be
supported by normal historical evidence and may therefore
be wrong, but it also seems to rule out the possibility that
his subject was unique and thus to some extent it dehumanizes him. Frequently the psycho-historian's language betrays
the problem: psycho-historical works are often full of phrases
like "there is reason to suppose that," "we may assume that,"
"most likely he," "he must have," etc.[3]

As one might expect, opposition to these new styles of
history has come from the more traditional practitioners.
Jacques Barzun, for example, widely known for his scathing
condemnation of *Webster's Third New International Dictionary,* studied the merits of psycho-history and concluded, not
surprisingly, that the behavioral techniques contributed no
valuable new historical insights.[4] Furthermore, he observed
that they contributed greatly to the reprehensible tendency
to use jargon in historical writing. Other critics have revived
the old argument of whether history is an art or a science.[5]
Should historians, they ask, work for scientific generalizations
at all? Is not the historian's task primarily the reconstruction
and illumination of the unique, of the particular? Does not
history militate against generalizations by its very nature?
Still others have expressed concern that the traditional pur-

3. For examples, see the review article by Hans W. Gatzke, "Hitler
and Psychohistory," *American Historical Review,* LXXVIII, 2 (April
1973), 394-401, esp. 398-399.
4. Jacques Barzun, "History: The Muse and her Doctors," *American
Historical Review,* LXXVII, 1 (February 1972), 36-64.
5. See e.g., David Herbert Donald, "Between Science and Art," *American Historical Review,* LXXVII, 2 (April 1972), 445-452.

poses for writing history are being neglected. The new hyphenated historians are no longer concerned with putting present society in touch with its past. Their works are written not for the general public but for fellow specialists. In fact, these works are increasingly becoming unreadable by the general public. Articles on social history are often replete with graphs, charts, and tables, and the works employing psychological techniques tend to be heavily jargon-ridden. It is indeed discouraging for an old-fashioned historian to stumble over phrases like "the evocation of a proxy," "aggressive and regressive behavior," "phallic-narcissistic character," or "reaction formation" in a journal article about that most political of creatures, Otto von Bismarck.[6] Put in other words, if historians become social scientists, will they not inevitably lose the old humanist keeper-of-the-traditions role?

Perhaps more significant than the negative reactions to socio- and psycho-history has been the willingness of some older, established historians to take the claims of the new hyphenated types of history seriously and to simply plead for a responsible use of the new techniques. Do not, they warn, write quantitative history until you are as knowledgeable about the use and limitations of statistics as the sociologists, economists, and political scientists are. Do not attempt psycho-history until you are up-to-date on all the various current psychological theories and are sure that you are not merely adding psychological jargon to common-sense observations. In fact, some of the older, established historians are trying their hand at it. The psychological phrases repeated above came from a recent article by the prominent German historian and Bismarck scholar Otto Pflanze, entitled "Toward a Psychoanalytic Interpretation of Bismarck."

Where will it all lead? Perhaps the old academic divisions in the social sciences and humanities are becoming obsolete. A time may be coming when we will no longer be able to categorize a scholar as a political scientist, economist, sociologist, or historian. Perhaps the discipline of history will lose its distinctiveness and finally become one of the social sciences.

6. Otto Pflanze, "Toward a Psychoanalytic Interpretation of Bismarck," *American Historical Review*, LXXVII, 2 (April 1972), 419-452.

One quantitative historian confidently predicts just such a consequence:

> The leading historians of more recent vintage are "historians' historians." It might be mentioned that we are only beginning work in quantitative history and in the use of the computer for historical research. If one asks, therefore, what the future holds, the answer I think must be that the present tendencies will continue and perhaps accelerate. The results of research will emerge in the form of an internal dialogue among scholars. The gap between the products of historical scholarship and the educated public will widen. History will undergo a development from which it was believed to be exempt, the same development that has taken place in most other fields of knowledge.[7]

But I for one still have immense sympathy for the notion that history is to serve present society as its cultural memory, and that this can best be achieved by carefully reconstructing past epochs and events in their full variety and complexity, by artistically telling the stories, and by writing it all in ordinary, jargon-free language for the general reading public. It is in this context that I can best understand my task as a Christian historian teaching Christian students. This is not to say, of course, that Christians ought not practice the new varieties of history or that Christian historians and other traditional historians cannot profit from the work of quantitative historians or psycho-historians. The new varieties of history can certainly help us make more accurate generalizations about past human behavior, especially about the usually nameless masses. We cannot teach or write history without generalizations — they are the necessary scaffolding — and any attempt to make them more reliable or scientific should be encouraged. But let's not confuse the scaffolding with the building. Generalizations must lead back to and finally yield to the particulars; otherwise they dehumanize and distort historical reality. In other words, let's not lose sight of the object of our discipline, man's past in all its richness and variety, or the purpose of our work — to remind living humans

7. Felix Gilbert and Stephen Graubard, *Historical Studies Today* (New York, 1972), p. xvii.

who they are and how they got that way. This task is, if anything, even more important for Christians than for secular
humanists. Christianity is after all an historical religion. Our
faith rests on certain specific historical events: Christ's birth,
ministry, death, and resurrection are part of history, as are
the founding of his church and its preservation. Telling the
stories and getting them straight is therefore exceedingly important to the Christian community.

If historical studies in the future become less distinguish-
able from the social sciences, I can only hope that some re-
searchers and teachers will continue to accept the traditional
vision and method of history so that the task will still be
performed. On the other hand, despite current enthusiasms
for the new varieties of history, the great majority of books
and articles written by historians seems to be fairly traditional
stuff. Perhaps the new varieties will become useful subdivi-
sions of history, integrated into the discipline without threat-
ening its traditional identity or purpose.[8] I hope so. In either
case, I would expect Christians to be prominent among those
concerned to preserve that identity and purpose.

8. The most recent writings on this subject by quantitative historians
already suggest a more moderate and modest assessment of their contribu-
tion and relationship to historical studies. For example, see Robert W.
Fogel, "The Limits of Quantitative Methods in History," *The American
Historical Review*, 80, 2 (April, 1975), 329-350 and Charlotte Erikson,
"Quantitative History," *ibid.*, 351-365. For a comprehensive survey of
recent quantitative studies in American History, see Robert P. Swierenga,
"Computers and American History: The Impact of the 'New' Generation,"
Journal of American History, 60 (1974), 1045-70.

Herbert Butterfield: The Legacy of a Christian Historian

WILLIAM A. SPECK

WITH THE ADVENT of a secular and scientific historiography, one might reasonably have expected the virtual disappearance of the Christian historian, who traditionally used explicit assumptions of faith in performing a discernible religious function. And, indeed, leading historians of the nineteenth century like Ranke, who were still believers, nevertheless largely secularized the task of the Christian historian. Although they were partly inspired by religious ideas, they kept them in the background. With few exceptions, they left to philosophers and theologians questions regarding morality, values, ultimate interpretations — the whole problem of reconciling faith and history. In practice, therefore, they were empirical investigators seeking mundane explanations to the larger themes of man's political and social development. In short, their work differed little from that of secular historians. The abandonment of an explicit religious role by the Christian historian seemed to be a well-established pattern until the middle third of this century, when against the background of crisis and theological renaissance, a number of notable scholars revived that role.

No one figures more prominently in this revival than Sir Herbert Butterfield, formerly Regius Professor of Modern History at Cambridge University. A scholar of outstanding merit and one with outspoken Christian convictions, Sir Herbert has developed a diverse religious role — obvious in his apologetic writings, but also evident in his pronouncements as a moralist and social critic. Christian assumptions have even affected his understanding and execution of academic history. Though his various undertakings, from apologist to professional historian, have found expression in disparate publications, he has worked with common purposes and

99

motifs. He has aimed to defend tradition, to revise and supplement a purely secular and — in his mind — an increasingly materialistic historiography, and to deal with fundamental problems. In each of his tasks, he has tried to demonstrate the compatibility of biblical ideas with the historical
approach, to show in fact how both are necessary in the
study and interpretation of human experience and human
problems. Finally, running through Sir Herbert's work are a
number of distinctive themes: among these are providence,
charity, and, above all, personality. Much of his thought has
been shaped by a Christian personalism that accords ultimate
significance and reality to individual personality. It is Sir
Herbert's versatility, his peculiar thematic unity and emphasis, and his manner of reconciling private belief with professional task that chiefly distinguish his achievement as a
Christian historian. Only Kenneth Scott Latourette and
Christopher Dawson have done as much to revive the tradition of the Christian historian. The survey of Sir Herbert's
religious role presented in this paper is based not only on his
published work but also on a personal interview that I conducted and taped.[1]

First, a few words about Sir Herbert's background. A
native of Yorkshire born in 1900, he acquired a living religious
faith chiefly from his father, a devout Methodist. During his
years in secondary school he developed a liking for history,
the study of which he continued at Cambridge. Though he
seriously considered a career in the Methodist ministry, the
forces drawing him to scholarship and teaching were stronger.
Therefore, until his retirement in 1968, he remained in Cambridge where in addition to his professorship he became
Master of Peterhouse and, for a brief term, vice-chancellor
of the university. In choosing an academic career and in fact
in making decisions throughout his life, he has felt himself
guided by providence. He has never abandoned a religious
vocation, for he has been a spokesman for his faith not only
as a Christian historian but also as a lay preacher for the

1. The interview took place on September 12-13, 1973. I wish to ex-
press my gratitude to the University of South Alabama Research
Committee, whose financial aid made my trip to Cambridge possible.

Methodist Church (until the late 1930s). Though living in retirement, Sir Herbert still maintains a busy schedule of lecturing, writing, and attending conferences; in his leisure time he pursues his favorite diversion — playing the piano. A short, slender, and silver-haired man, he revealed during the two days I spent with him the personal qualities that have shaped his life and work. Although he takes his vocation and beliefs seriously, he is notably cheerful, unassuming, and tolerant. As an advocate and critic, he has avoided acrimony and arrogance, seeking instead to persuade and reconcile. A spirit of moderation has thus set the tone for his activity as a Christian historian.

In examining Sir Herbert's religious role, we must bear in mind that during the first half of his career, until the Second World War, he kept religious views out of his writings. Thus he did not begin his life's work with a preconceived plan for reconciling faith and history. On the contrary, he seemed to be practicing his craft in the manner of any other serious scholar until 1944, when, near the end of *The Englishman and His History*, he revealed a Christian concern for what he considered the tragic course of contemporary events.[2] The movement from technical historian to Christian historian was more dramatically and decisively signaled by his agreement, secured only after considerable coaxing by others, to deliver a series of lectures in Cambridge on the theological significance of history. The widely acclaimed results were published as *Christianity and History*,[3] perhaps the single most distinguished statement by a twentieth-century Christian historian. Encouraged by the success of his lectures, Sir Herbert proceeded thereafter in a more deliberate fashion to advance religious interpretations.

If we are to understand his distinctive role as a Christian historian, we must begin by considering his first principles — the heart of his position as an apologist. Unlike many defenders of a Christian interpretation of history, he does not present the usual recitation of salvation events climaxed by the Incarnation; nor does he focus upon the life of the church. While

2. Hamden, Conn., 1970.
3. New York, 1950.

he accepts the Incarnation as the pivotal event in history, and appreciates the redemptive work of the church, he has preferred to relate sacred history to secular history in a different way. His thoughts on the subject were not prompted by a particular school of theology, but were, as he told me, the product of "Bible-reading and doing history."

Sir Herbert's special emphasis falls on a biblical doctrine of man and providence. His most fundamental assertions defend, sometimes in eloquent terms, the dignity and value of man. "Human beings, though fallen from the state of innocence, move as gods and bear the image of God. . . . Each is a precious jewel, each a separate well of life, each we may say a separate poem."[4] Human personalities "are the crowning blossom of creation";[5] and, accordingly, the purpose of history is "the manufacture and education of human souls."[6] "Actual live human beings are to be taken as the values in the world because they are souls meant for eternity."[7] And finally: "We envisage our history in the proper light, therefore, if we say that each generation — indeed each individual — exists for the glory of God."[8] Sir Herbert's personalism gives man a central place in determining the course of events. In *Christianity and History* we find the following metaphor: history is a symphony in which human beings are free to play what they wish in the orchestra, while God the composer works to create harmony and design the notes already played (pp. 94-95). In other words, man makes history in the short run, but the long-range results are in the hands of the Almighty.

Sir Herbert's metaphor provides for God's orderings in history, manifested in providential sustenance, judgment, and grace. "There is a Providence that we must regard as lying in the very constitution of things" (p. 95). It upholds the order in which man finds himself. And as divine government, providence engages in a history-making that happens over the

4. *The Englishman*, p. 133.
5. *Christianity and History*, p. 28.
6. *Ibid.*, p. 76.
7. *History and Human Relations* (New York, 1952), p. 50.
8. *Christianity and History*, p. 67.

heads of human beings. Ideally, man should cooperate with providence by seeking the good and practicing charity in his small corner of the universe. Unfortunately, he has often acted otherwise, elevating himself to the position of sovereign maker of history in sinful rebellion against God. Providential judgment falls hardest upon those who, like the Germans in this century, overreach themselves. Yet, owing to man's cupidity and presumption, all civilizations, nations, and institutions suffer a similar fate. Indeed, the world wars and revolutions of our time are, Sir Herbert suggested to me, judgments on an entire civilization. How does one explain undeserved suffering? Sir Herbert has no neat answer, but believes man has considerable freedom to defy providence, to cause widespread misery. Moreover, in some cases — for example, ancient Israel — suffering has a redemptive purpose, and thus we have the biblical figure of the suffering servant. That figure as applied to Christ discloses subsequent redemptive activity in history.

More broadly, Sir Herbert refers in *Christianity and History* to providential grace, the workings of a "reconciling mind," a "superintending intellect," or the "collective wisdom of the human race" (pp. 98-99). This kind of grace, which lies in the structure of history, functions to provide renewal and reconstruction in times of disintegration and destruction, to repair the mistakes of the past, and to turn disaster and evil into something positive and good. Providence was at work when the fire of London prepared the way for a thoughtful and aesthetic reconstruction; when religious wars led to toleration; when the American Revolution convinced the English to adopt a more progressive colonial policy. In Sir Herbert's view, providential grace in large measure accounts for the possibility of genuine human and social progress. He writes: "Providence produces a world in which men can live and gradually improve their external conditions, in spite of sin — in other words it does the best that human beings have left possible for it at any time" (p. 34).

For Sir Herbert, biblical doctrines of man and providence, though based on faith, illuminate and explain historical processes to a considerable degree: the central role of man; the presence of evil, conflict, and disaster; cycles of nemesis and good fortune; periodic human renewal; and the gains of civilization. Even so, a validation of the Christian view is not to be found in a survey of the ages but in the effect of that view on human personality, more visible to the biographer than to the historian, more real to the believer than to the nonbeliever. Despite the supporting testimony of history and even the biblical record, decisions regarding ultimate interpretations are not a matter of scholarship but of faith, a faith growing out of self-analysis, the "actual experience of life" (p. 21).

For this and other reasons, Sir Herbert believes that ordinary historical writing is an inappropriate vehicle for trying to demonstrate the Christian thesis.[9] Nothing could be further from his mind when he engages in the practice of his discipline than attempting such a demonstration. The defense of a theology of history is one matter; the actual doing of conventional narrative and analysis is quite another. An empirical study demands concrete evidence and warranted inferences, and so long as Sir Herbert does this kind of study he follows the rules and seeks to convince people of widely different persuasions. As he understands it, the aim of technical history is scientific and limited: to show what can be established by the observable data. The historian is guilty of intellectual arrogance if he tries to assert more than the evidence permits. Thus he is in no position to decide "the quality of Beethoven's music, the rightness of the Reformation, and the question of the divinity of Christ."[10] Least of all can he claim to find in his study the overall meaning of the human drama. So, with the coming of the scientific age in historiography, Sir Herbert sees the need as a Christian to write history at different levels: only at the level of general interpretation does he think it permissible to introduce personal

9. Sir Herbert discusses the relationship between Christianity and historical scholarship in *Christianity and History,* chapter 1, and in "The Christian and Historical Study," *History and Human Relations,* pp. 131-157. For a detailed examination of his views on the subject, see William A. Speck, "Herbert Butterfield on the Christian and Historical Study," *Fides et Historia,* IV (Fall 1971), 50-70.
10. *Human Relations,* p. 135.

philosophical or religious views. This means that he has abandoned the attempt to integrate judgments of faith and factual analysis in a conventional historical study. He indicated to me that he saw no way of accomplishing such integration even if it were desirable. For after all, assertions of belief would not only compromise professional standards but would seem to have little or no utility in a typical monographic study.

If Sir Herbert draws a sharp line of demarcation between academic history and Christian interpretation, he nonetheless shows how the working historian can still take religious preconceptions to his task, how he can use them to define and conduct that task. Over the years Sir Herbert has gradually come to realize that even an empirical study in effect serves Christian purposes, incorporates spiritual ideals in secular form, owes its existence in part to biblical religion, for which temporal events have crucial importance. He sees historical study as working to a Christian purpose because its highest object is to promote human understanding. Moreover, he perceives in much historical writing an expression of Christian personalism. Traditional narrative does several things: it shows an interest in individuals and past generations for their own sake; it portrays the human drama as an affair of individual personalities, endowed with self-consciousness, freedom, and intellect; it reveals in the minute investigations of day-by-day events the uniqueness and unpredictability of individual actions; it takes seriously the creative, artistic, and spiritual side of personality; it thus underscores the fact that things happen in history because men have vitality, make plans, and take actions. Because circumstances of time and place condition rather than determine human behavior, historical events cannot be mechanically and externally explained but must be traced to personalities, to "mind and motive, hope and fear, passion and faith."[11] That being the case, the proper study of the past demands not only a story of what men did but also the exercise of Christian charity in the form of sympathetic imagination, the attempt to gain an interior knowl-

11. *Christianity and History*, p. 26.

edge of someone unlike ourselves and to interpret contrasting personalities fairly.

According to Sir Herbert, when the historian turns from narrative to analysis and examines factors conditioning human action, he still engages in an activity resembling a religious task. For example, he is practicing a mode of charity when he makes allowances for people and thus he is inclined not to blame them the more he appreciates how much they are influenced by historical forces. Although the concept of human freedom and responsibility is hardly erased by the realization of conditioning factors, the point is that any sound assessment of that responsibility must take into account the considerable degree to which man is the creature — even the victim — of the past, how much in theological language his case even calls for something like forgiveness, though a forgiveness he cannot claim to deserve. The study of the operation of necessity in the historical process also has deep significance for Sir Herbert because for him it is also the study of the structure of the providential order with its regularities and laws. Although he fully recognizes the material setting of life, the effect of long-range developments, and the influence of the total society and culture on the individual,[12] he does not want us to lose sight of a danger in contemporary historiography: the greater use of social scientific investigations of problems, structures, patterns, while valid and valuable, can easily obscure the role of personality, can cause us to forget the need for narrative history, can lead to a deterministic view of things. Sir Herbert has consistently opposed any historical methodology that seems to reduce men and ideas to epiphenomena, mere by-products of their age, mere functions and rationalizations of vested interests.[13]

Both religious and professional convictions have reinforced his own preference for a traditional history. The titles of his major studies clearly indicate this: *The Peace Tactics*

12. See "History of Europe," *Chambers' Encyclopedia*, 1949.
13. See "Marxist History," in *History and Human Relations*, pp. 66-100; "George III and the Namier School," in *George III and the Historians*, rev. ed. (New York, 1959), pp. 193-299.

of Napoleon, 1806-1808;[14] The Statecraft of Machiavelli;[15] George III, Lord North and the People, 1779-1780;[16] The Origins of Modern Science, 1300-1800;[17] and numerous works on the history of historiography, including Man on His Past.[18] These writings reflect his conviction that men, individually as in the case of a Galileo or a Napoleon, or in small dedicated groups like the early Christians or the Bolsheviks, can alter the course of history.[19] At the same time, these books indicate the importance of ideas, particularly the role played by science and historiography in creating the modern mind. Even though secular subjects form the bulk of Sir Herbert's work, they have never been divorced in his mind from the background of Christian civilization. Indeed, he sees the movements associated with modern science and historiography as the consequences in part of a desire to achieve a more accurate description of the providential order in nature and time.[20]

In discussing the effect of Christianity on civilization, Sir Herbert reveals still another religious aspect of his academic task.[21] Although the point does not occupy a prominent place in his historiography, he believes that "the grand fact of European history is the constant preaching of the gospel, the conversion of souls to a more authentic appropriation of religion, and the ministering to their spiritual necessities."[22] Aside from its inestimable effect on individuals over the centuries, Christianity has acted as a leaven in society as a whole. Its ideals fostered — if the established church did

14. Cambridge, 1929.
15. London, 1940.
16. London, 1949.
17. New York, 1951.
18. Cambridge, 1955.
19. See "The Role of the Individual in History," History, XL (February, June 1955), 1-17.
20. Sir Herbert has considered the religious dimensions of historiography in his Gifford Lectures of 1965-66. He is presently preparing a major study based on those lectures, which are as yet unpublished. In the meantime, see his recent essay "Historiography," in Dictionary of the History of Ideas, ed. Philip P. Wiener (New York, 1973), II, 464-98.
21. See Christianity in European History (London, 1952); "Christianity in History," in Dictionary of the History of Ideas, I, 373-412.
22. "The Christian and the Ecclesiastical Interpretation of History," Christian Newsletter, July 6, 1949, p. 226.

not — the development of humanitarianism, democracy, socialism, and internationalism. Above all, a spiritual definition of
man has been the most important single historical source of
respect for personality and individual rights achieved in the
Western world. If Sir Herbert believes that a secular age
needs to be reminded of its religious foundations, as a technical historian he does not proceed beyond that point. In
any case, the vindication of the faith is not to be found in its
mundane by-products. Narrative and analysis are for Sir
Herbert a Christian task not because they furnish evidence
for the apologist but because their aims and nature are to a
considerable degree harmonious with religious principles and
because in their practice the believer in particular should
"remember the limits of the science, the need for humility of
mind, the importance of getting inside human beings, the
call for charity, the dynamic quality of the spiritual factor in
history."[23]

As a Christian historian, Sir Herbert also believes he has
a moral function; yet he has been a moralist in a very special
sense. At the center of his attention is the question of moral
judgments; no other subject has stirred his deepest convictions more. Beginning with *The Whig Interpretation of History*,[24] he has tried to work out a position in conformity with
faith and historical scholarship — in particular one that does
justice to his view of human personality. He has criticized
contemporary trends in thought that endanger that conception. In our conversation he spoke of his profound objection
to "that modern outlook which practically takes away human
responsibility altogether and assumes that human sins and
crimes can be explained away." He continued by noting that
"you are unmanning the person, you are depersonalizing him
if you say he has no responsibility at all. It would be a dis-
service to human personality generally." Sir Herbert is a traditional moralist up to a point, because he believes in definite
standards of right and wrong, affirms man's freedom and moral

23. *Human Relations*, p. 156.
24. London, 1931. Also see his important essay on moral judgments in
Human Relations.

responsibility, recognizes a real struggle between good and evil, and asserts man's general culpability.

In other ways, however, he departs from tradition. Although he defends the validity of universal judgments — all men are sinners, all societies are corrupt — he deplores a moralism that passes judgment on specific individuals or that damns specific political and social systems, nations, religions, and the like. Even a Hitler or a totalitarian regime should not be singled out for moral censure (is either uniquely or totally evil?). While Sir Herbert feels justified in denouncing immoral actions or opposing political repression, he does not wish to judge the perpetrators: thus he condemns sin but not the sinner. He thinks God alone can determine the degree of moral responsibility in individual cases, can make final assessments of people. Moreover, Sir Herbert argues that the passing of moral judgments on human personality is compatible neither with Christian charity nor with the historian's chief aim of understanding man within the context of his particular time and place. In the course of describing events, the historian may well have to recount the apparent misdeeds of individuals and countries; but moral judgments directed against those individuals and countries interfere with the practice of sympathetic imagination and obscure the role of purely historical causes. Such judgments encourage moralistic interpretations of events, featuring a simplistic and melodramatic contest between the righteous and the unrighteous.

But history, according to Sir Herbert, is not the story of good people locked in conflict with bad people: struggles between Protestants and Catholics, Whigs and Tories, Communists and non-Communists must be seen as encounters between sinners and other sinners. (The drama of good versus evil is played out within individual personalities.) If the Nazis and Communists committed excesses and atrocities clearly distinguishing them from democratic leadership, it was not simply because of innate human wickedness or even extraordinary human perversity, but rather because of moral failure greatly encouraged by conditions of adversity: the Nazis and Communists were acting in a setting where civilized restraints and safeguards had been weakened by war, revolution, economic dislocation, or dictatorship — external circumstances that bring the worst out of people, so to speak. Although they are still responsible for not doing better in those circumstances, what person can be sure that he would have acted differently in their place? Thus, even though one leader or one regime might be more evil in practice than another, differences between men and systems should be attributed in large part to the effect of historical forces working on human nature. The basic distinction Sir Herbert draws between democracies and totalitarian states is not moral but sociological: that is, the first are more highly civilized than the second. This distinction is of course crucial, and no one prizes order and liberty more than Sir Herbert.[25] Yet the democracies may not adopt a self-righteous stance, may not claim an inherent moral superiority for their citizenries. They have often acted immorally themselves (racism, imperialism, etc.); besides, their strong points and advantages are derived to a considerable degree from favorable traditions and stable conditions. For these reasons, Sir Herbert tends to lump all countries into the same moral category. When asked whether present-day Communism is not a clear negation of Christianity, he replied, "Not any more than all mundane systems."

Sir Herbert takes literally the biblical injunctions to refrain from judging and to practice charity. He accepts the proposition that we are all too much tainted by evil ourselves to sit in judgment on others. In interpreting past or present political conflict, he is in the last instance guided by the belief that "no law of God or man, and no alleged utility, can supersede the law or transcend the utility of extending charity to all men, or can set imaginable limits to the law of charity" (*Human Relations*, p. 112). As a moralist, Sir Herbert wishes to put into operation, therefore, the following basic rule of Christian conduct: "We should judge all men to be sinners but treat all men as born for eternity" (p. 55).

Sir Herbert points out that, unfortunately, this rule has been too often violated in our time. Men have used moral judgments to justify hatred and aggression, with disastrous effects. Those judgments form part of the general crisis confronting

25. See *Liberty in the Modern World* (Toronto, 1952).

the world since 1914, which Sir Herbert has examined from a religious-historical perspective in various writings, particularly *Christianity, Diplomacy and War*[26] and *International Conflict in the Twentieth Century*.[27] The crisis is not defined simply as the blindness of moral judgments but rather by a whole host of intellectual errors — mistaken views of man, society, and history generated by secularization and social conflict. Sir Herbert criticizes those views severely not only because they contradict Christian truth but also because they have done severe damage to the life of humanity.

What are the errors in question? They are the belief in the natural goodness of man and in the possibility of utopia; an individualism that enthrones the ego and its inversion in a collectivism that identifies society as the real personality; a deterministic and naturalistic conception of man, or a conception that turns him into a means to an end; a moralism and self-righteousness manifested in political ideologies that dismiss opponents as the final seat of evil, deserving of extermination. These ideas have been influential and widely held. Sir Herbert cites as examples not only fascism and Communism but also militant anti-Communism; not only German nationalism but also American nationalism; not only socialism but also capitalism. While Sir Herbert sees the worst consequences of these intellectual errors under a Stalin or Hitler, he detects a general falling away from traditional notions of God and man. This century has witnessed the following results: (1) the subordination of personality to country, party, economic process, or some other mundane end; (2) the dehumanization of one's rivals, which is in essence the "failure to respect the other man's personality";[28] (3) persecutions, atrocities, and internal and external wars for righteousness (e.g., to wipe out the "evil" capitalists or the Viet Cong).

All these consequences flow from a spiritual deficiency, namely, the failure to see and treat one's fellow man as a

26. New York, 1953.
27. New York, 1960. Elements of his social criticism also appear in *Christianity and History* and in *Christianity in European History*. For a more recent statement, see "Christianity and Politics," *Orbis*, X (Winter 1967), 1233-46.
28. *Christianity, Diplomacy and War*, p. 49.

creature of God possessing infinite worth. In other words, even though Communism and democracy may both stand for high ideals, may both profess to advance the cause of humanity, they too easily fail in practice because they lack a spiritual foundation, the view that human beings exist for the glory of God and are subordinate only to him. Sir Herbert does not expect the world to adopt suddenly his Christian personalism, but he does feel that improvements in domestic and international politics depend in part on an increase in respect for human personality. He has repeatedly argued that a primary condition of détente is a toning down of self-righteousness and an opening to the "realization that the members of whatever may be the hostile party are human beings too, not fundamentally unlike ourselves."[29] He calls first for a scientific (historical) — in contrast to a moralistic — interpretation of political conflict and, second, a charity that respects human personality, a catholicity of mind that embraces different races, nations, and political systems. They both can contribute to the most important goal of diplomacy, the maintenance of an international order that permits and protects diverse regimes and ideologies.

Although Sir Herbert has sharply criticized his time, has underscored intellectual errors, human sinfulness, divine judgment, he is not a cultural pessimist yearning for the restoration of an ideal past. If he is aware of a serious crisis, he is also aware of significant progress. Advances exist side by side with setbacks, and the violation of human personality has been partly offset by efforts to improve the conditions of life. In our meeting, Sir Herbert expressed considerable optimism about the future and called attention to his belief in progress, a belief much more evident now than in the years immediately after World War II. Modern man, in his view, has made material, intellectual, and scientific advances generally improving the human lot; and, even in the midst of threats to personality, man has in some ways progressed morally (note the increased regard for women, children, workers, minorities, and the social reforms elevating their status). In the

29. *International Conflict in the Twentieth Century*, p. 68.

sense of transposing attitudes from religion to society at large, secularization has had, therefore, a beneficial effect. Even secularization as referring to the church's loss of institutional and ideological predominance can be seen as a gain. The religious uniformity of the past was enforced by custom and command, preventing what is really a Christian ideal — freedom of conscience. Established churches often abused their power, provoking resentment against religion as well as against ecclesiastical authority. Sir Herbert believes that the return today to what he calls "New Testament conditions" is to be welcomed, because the decision to be a Christian is no longer forced or affected as much by nonspiritual inducements: that decision is more likely to stem from personal experience. In order to thrive, the church does not need power, wealth, or privilege, but only a world in which people enjoy religious freedom.

How does Sir Herbert envision the responsibility of the contemporary church? We discussed this issue at length. Sir Herbert believes that Christians can contribute most, not by pursuing mundane goals, but by nurturing the spiritual life. Any kind of political theology that allows for or advocates violent measures is "knocking the New Testament on its head" ("Christ wouldn't allow the sword"): this makes the mundane things the end and Christianity only the means. Even if revolution might be justified in extraordinary cases ("the most justifiable revolution that ever occurred was the Russian one"), the mechanics of revolution lead to times of terror. The proper role of the church is to steer an independent course, being tied neither to the regime nor to the cause of the antiregime. The effects of Christianity on the world in the past have been produced not by a deliberate strategy to overturn the established order but by an indirect process, as the by-product of Christian living. Christians can best fight evil by preaching the gospel and practicing charity. Sir Herbert thinks that "Christians out to be otherworldly have a colossal effect on the world." He has written that "those who preach the Gospel, nurse the pieties, spread New Testament Love, and affirm the spiritual nature of man are guarding the very fountain, dealing with the problems of civilization at its very source, and keeping open the spring from which new things will still arise."[30]

In our conversation, Sir Herbert predicted a large future role for the Christian faith. While deeply concerned by the challenge of secular society to religion, he thinks that in the long run such a society will prove highly vulnerable to the Christian message because it lacks the means by which to satisfy man's spiritual needs. Less vulnerable will be the other high religions. Yet, the groundwork for Christian advances against secularism as well as other faiths has already been laid: "I think that world history is going to be different because of the last hundred years of missionary work by the church."

Has Sir Herbert himself contributed to the anticipated future success of Christianity? Certainly he has tried to enhance the intellectual respectability of his faith for contemporaries, apparently with some success: *Christianity and History,* translated into eight languages, has enjoyed a wide readership. Perhaps it is more important in assessing his achievement to note the large part he has played in making the Christian historian more respectable. He has been a central figure in the twentieth-century revival of the Christian historian who practices an explicitly religious role. How should we evaluate his work?

Sir Herbert has clearly shown the feasibility of a religious role for contemporary scholars. The Christian historian need not be a mere technician completely governed by secular assumptions, nor does he have to compromise academic standards in order to assert a religious perspective. Sir Herbert's work reveals a method useful to the typical researcher whose specialty or professional reservations prevent him from mixing judgments of faith and historical explanation within the framework of a conventional study, such as was done by Latourette in his church histories. For historians in other fields like himself, Sir Herbert has developed what is probably the most acceptable and workable procedure for practicing both a scholarly and a religious role, for turning academic history into a Christian task, for supplementing secular history with

30. *Christianity in European History,* p. 55.

theological interpretation, completing the investigation of events begun by empirical research. In essence, his method consists in this: drawing on the resources of scholarship and faith in writing history at different levels, moving from technical studies to theology of history.

Sir Herbert's writings reveal not only a procedure but also an agenda of tasks for the Christian historian, a program of historical revision and religious advocacy. More completely than anyone else, he has illustrated the variety of a religious role. He has tried to show the theological significance of time, the uniqueness of the Christian achievement, the causal importance of moral and religious factors, and the spiritual roots of contemporary problems. In addition, he has investigated the ways in which ancient Judaism and the Christian religion helped to shape the character of history as it came to develop in the Western world. Finally, he has defended the relevance of traditional values in contemporary life. We can summarize these activities by saying that Sir Herbert in defending religion has exercised an apologetic function; in criticizing his time he has performed something of a prophetic function. In both cases, he has aimed not only to challenge the assumptions and interpretations of secular historiography but also to act as a Christian spokesman addressing himself to vital issues for the general public.

How well has Sir Herbert carried out his religious role? How successfully has he reconciled faith and history? How convincing are his ideas? Let us briefly consider his contributions, raising critical questions at the same time. We can well appreciate the dialectical quality of Sir Herbert's thought because it takes into account the complexity of existence, with its good and evil, freedom and necessity, judgment and grace, progress and decline, and the like. Yet, has he always assigned the proper weight to the factors making up that complexity? Take, for example, his theory of historical causation: is his metaphor of the symphony and the composer theologically sound if it turns God into a divine improviser struggling to repair man's mistakes? And is man really the fountainhead of events to the degree Sir Herbert thinks, if man is so easily swayed by external circumstances, not to mention his own defective nature? In this connection, can Sir Herbert rightly ignore the psychological roots (e.g., neurosis) of human behavior? We can welcome Sir Herbert's revival of a doctrine of providence, too frequently ignored in our time. Yet, is that doctrine, unaccompanied by a doctrine of Christ, the church, and the parousia, an adequate basis for a Christian interpretation of history? We may see in Sir Herbert's personalism a necessary corrective to a collectivist and violent age. But is the dignity of man properly supported in a theology (as presented in *Christianity and History*) that gives more attention to his sinfulness and negative effect on history than to his creative, positive role — a theology that, in fact, attributes human progress chiefly to providence?

The following points should also be made. Sir Herbert has probably formulated the best possible argument against moral judgments. Even so, we still might wonder if the highest Christian ideals are really served if we suspend judgment in the case of individuals responsible for Vietnam, genocide, the preaching of hatred and violence? Moreover, while it is important to indicate the Christian basis of Western civilization as Sir Herbert does, is it not somewhat one-sided of him to trace most of the good things, from democracy to social reforms, to the influence of religious ideals and to imply that their survival depends on spiritual renewal? In discussing the role of faith in the West, Sir Herbert has, to be sure, made a valuable contribution by showing the religious origins and nature of historical writing. He has given us one of the few Christian interpretations of historical study itself. But, we might ask, does not the technical history that Sir Herbert finds compatible with Christian belief actually weaken religious particularism and moral absolutes, in effect feed a secular view of life? If we wish to talk about a clearly "Christian" historiography, do we not have to refer to something like Latourette's church histories or to Sir Herbert's own interpretive essays? To sum up, Sir Herbert's ideas can be assessed in the following way: although his thought has its lacunae and vulnerable points and thus does not provide us with a fully satisfactory reconciliation of faith and history, it does relate Christianity, often in a fresh and persuasive manner, to issues confronting the historian as well as the contemporary world.

What, then, is Sir Herbert's significance as a Christian historian? Probably more vividly than anyone else, he has demonstrated the feasibility, variety, and relevance of a religious role for the Christian historian. He has worked out a procedure and a program, and he offers examples of how to make effective use of familiar biblical concepts. In all these ways he has been a leader in revitalizing the tradition of Christian historian. The creation of a model for those wishing to continue that tradition may well prove to be Sir Herbert Butterfield's most enduring legacy.

Kenneth Scott Latourette's Vocation as Christian Historian

WILLIAM A. SPECK

THE CHRISTIAN HISTORIAN who tries to reconcile faith and history undertakes an imposing task. Two questions define his task: at the level of conventional historical study and writing, how can he function in accord with both religious faith and secular scholarship? At the level of general interpretation, how can he place in Christian perspective the past reconstructed by historiography? In this century, professional historians such as Sir Herbert Butterfield, Christopher Dawson, Gerhard Ritter, Henri Marrou, and Oscar Halecki took, in varying degrees, Christian assumptions to their work. Kenneth Scott Latourette (1884-1968) was probably the most notable American example. A distinguished Asian and church historian, he conducted his studies as a scientific investigator and as a professing Christian. His church historiography in particular represents an attempt to reconcile scholarly and religious commitments. This essay examines and evaluates that attempt.

The basic nature of Latourette's two commitments can be quickly stated.[1] As a man of scholarship, he was dedicated

---

1. Latourette discusses his private and professional convictions in the following: his autobiography, *Beyond the Ranges* (Grand Rapids, 1967); "My Guided Life," in *Frontiers of the Christian World Mission Since 1938: Essays in Honor of Kenneth Scott Latourette*, ed. Wilber Christian Harr (New York, 1962), pp. 281-293; "A History Teacher's Confession of Faith," *The Ohio History Teacher's Journal*, No. 19 (1920), 177-82; *A History of the Expansion of Christianity* (New York, 1937-45), I. "Introduction"; "The Christian Understanding of History," *American Historical Review*, LIV (1949), 259-76; an untitled statement in *What I Believe*, ed. Sir James Marchant (London, 1953), pp. 49-56; *What Can I Believe About Christian Missions?* (New York, 1931); "The Real Issue in Foreign Missions," *Christian Century*, April, 1931, pp. 506-8; "Every Christian a Missionary," *Criterion*, May, 1955, p. 3; *Challenge and Conformity: Studies in the Interaction of Christianity and the World Today* (New York, 1955), ch. 1.

to history for its own sake. In his appreciation of man's historical nature, he was "secular" to the degree that any serious scholar who wishes to study the past in an acceptable manner must be. At Yale he was trained in the school of "scientific" history, the assumptions of which he accepted with few reservations. In order to write the best history possible, he carried out an extensive and critical investigation into the sources. And he endeavored to present the facts and inferences based on them. As a man of faith, he belonged to the evangelical Protestant tradition that stressed conversion of individuals, personal piety, evangelism, and humanitarianism. He accepted literally the articles of faith enunciated in the Apostles' and Nicene Creeds. Belief in the gospel, personal rebirth, and missionary enthusiasm were the three essential phenomena of an authentic and vital Christianity. He was an historical and theological optimist, reflecting the high expectations of the age in which he attained maturity and a personal inclination to underscore the redemptive features of Christianity. Devout and puritan, he sought God's will for his life. As a result of his faith, he practiced and promoted evangelism in a variety of roles, from ordained Baptist minister and Bible study leader to mission board member and university professor. From his two closely related careers and commitments he drew the resources that shaped his historiography and historical thought.

He conceived that his overall professional task was to be an historian and a Christian. His historical purpose was highly practical: in examining the history of China and Christian missions, he was conscious that he was filling gaps left by other historians.[2] Much of his scholarly distinction lies in his early leadership as a Sinologist and missiologist. He also dealt with his subjects in a pragmatic fashion. History was not for him a mere exercise in literary expression, the recon-

2. Four early articles are pertinent: "The History of the Far East, a Neglected Field," *The History Teacher's Magazine,* June, 1916, pp. 183-85; "American Scholarship and Chinese History," *Journal of the American Oriental Society,* XXXVIII (1918), 97-106; "The Missionary Factor in Recent History," *The Ohio History Teacher's Journal,* No. 15 (1919), 102-9; "The Study of the History of Missions," *International Review of Missions,* January, 1925, pp. 108-15.

struction of different worlds in the past, or a detailed narrative dramatizing men and events. He wrote mainly for the sake of the present.[3] In his introductions to China and his surveys of Christianity, approximately half the space was given to historical background, the other half to the nineteenth and twentieth centuries. He wished to promote among a wide readership an elementary understanding of contemporary China and Christianity. *The Chinese: Their History and Culture*[4] and *A History of Christianity*,[5] for example, were intended for students and the general reader. Although his multi-volume *A History of the Expansion of Christianity*[6] as well as *Christianity in a Revolutionary Age*[7] were more obviously monuments of scholarship, they were meant to be helpful not only to specialists but also to those engaged in the work of the church. In this instance, his pragmatic approach served a Christian purpose.

Latourette also defined his general role in religious terms. He believed that his scholarly work constituted a specifically Christian vocation. His studies of China and Christianity were inspired by a sense of "Christian obligation" and "missionary purpose."[8] He felt called to help in the opening up of Chinese and missions history as new fields of research and teaching, the more so because of his brief experience in China as a missionary teacher.[9] At the same time, missionary zeal encouraged his selection of topics. "My writing," he declares in his autobiography, "was an outgrowth of the global outreach of the Christian faith."[10]

Latourette's conception of vocation also had roots in theological optimism. His work rested on the belief that *Weltgeschichte* was *Heilsgeschichte*: although the effort of God to save man "has centred and been climaxed in 'salvation history,'" he "has been active in all history, and in ways not

3. See "Teacher's Confession."
4. New York, 1964 (originally published by Macmillan in two volumes in 1934).
5. New York, 1953.
6. Grand Rapids (7 vols.).
7. Westport, Conn., 1973 (5 vols.).
8. *Beyond the Ranges,* p. 61.
9. "Guided Life," pp. 290-91.
10. *Beyond the Ranges,* p. 109.

inconsistent with 'salvation history,' properly understood."[11] For example, God has to some extent sought and influenced men through the agency of non-Christian religions.[12] Moreover, what appear to be ordinary events to the secular mind, capable of historical explanation, actually have theological meaning. For Latourette, in other words, historical study is at once the examination of a mundane order and a providential order. The latter is discernible: the pattern of progress and failure, spiritual and temporal, provides evidence for the historian, "which suggests a strong probability for the truth of the Christian understanding [of history]."[13]

Though Latourette believed God to be active in all of history, he considered that activity most easily discernible in the story of Christianity and its expansion. Consequently, he discusses the theological meaning of events in his church studies, but not in his East Asian studies. In the former, where his religious commitment is fully engaged, he reveals himself as a Christian historian. Part of his purpose is to show how the historic role of the church tends to confirm a Christian view of the course of events.

The working out of Latourette's pragmatic and religious purpose is closely tied to a revisionist interpretation of modern Christianity. He understood but strongly disagreed with the frequent labelling of the period since the French Revolution as "post-Christian." Since in his opinion Christianity is a young and growing force in the world, he felt that the period should be designated "pre-Christian."[14] Beginning with *Expansion*, his histories of the faith serve to demonstrate the following thesis:

> Christianity, beginning in a very unpromising fashion, has gone forward by a series of pulsations of advance, retreat, and advance. Each advance has carried the Christian tide farther than its predecessor, and each major recession has been shorter and less marked than the one

11. *Christianity Through the Ages* (New York, 1962), p. xi.
12. "An Appreciation of Non-Christian Faiths," *The World Tomorrow*, January, 1928, p. 25.
13. "Christian Understanding," p. 271.
14. See "The Present: Post-Christian or Pre-Christian," *Religion in Life*, XXXIII (1964), 170-79.

before it. . . . In the mid-twentieth century, if mankind is viewed as a whole, Christianity is more a force in the human scene than it or any other religion has ever been.[15]

The life of Jesus Christ "is the most influential ever lived on this planet and its effect continues to mount. Here is the most thought-provoking fact of human history."[16]

For Latourette this thesis possesses both historical and theological significance. Accordingly, he maintains that his study raises two sets of questions. The first confronts the historian. Why has Christianity spread? By what processes has it spread? What have been its human and cultural consequences? Why does it continue to advance and yet suffer setbacks? Why has the life of Jesus been the "most influential ever lived on this planet"? The history of Christianity also poses and sheds light on questions for the theologian. Does history have a meaning? If so, what is it?[17] Did God act uniquely in Jesus, sending him into the world in order to save it?[18] Will God achieve all his purposes within history?[19] As a Christian historian, Latourette seeks to answer both sets of questions.

To carry out his task, he uses a methodology derived from historical science and Christian belief. First and foremost, his working principles and procedures are shaped by the imperative to write reliable history. Without a solid basis of historical knowledge there can be no adequate comprehension of Christianity, no accurate description of either the temporal or the providential order, no intelligent Christian interpretation of the past. He aims to investigate the "mechanical and human factors" operating in culture and influencing the flow of events. Those factors he lists as the "geographical, climatic, economic, political, social, aesthetic, and intellectual."

15. *Revolutionary Age*, V, 534. Cf. *The Unquenchable Light* (New York, 1941), pp. xv-xviii, 171; *Expansion*, VII, 493-94; *A History of Christianity*, p. 1471. Latourette held to this thesis until the end. See "Christian Missions and the Changing World," *Review and Expositor*, LXII (1965), 163-74; "The Christian World Mission," *Baptist Watchman-Examiner*, December 26, 1968, pp. 806-7.
16. *A History of Christianity*, p. 34.
17. *Expansion*, VII, 483.
18. *A History of Christianity*, p. 60.
19. *Revolutionary Age*, I, 5.

He looks for causes "in preceding events, in human nature, and in the physical environment."[20] In accordance with his training, he also strives for objectivity — within the limitations of his value system. He cites as ideal working principles "carefulness of statement," "catholicity of mind," "judgment and balance," and "an absolute fearlessness in facing facts."[21] More than once he declares himself eager to discover what actually happened in the past.[22]

Latourette's methodology is secular and scientific only in a restricted sense. His secularity and objectivity are limited by a personal bias, by an expansionist view of Christianity, and by the decision to speak occasionally as a believer, in order, for example, to call attention to facts incapable of purely historical explanation.[23] During the writing of *Expansion*, he abandoned his initial intention of avoiding any attempt to prove a thesis and any discussion of the "cosmic significance" of events (pp. xvi, xxii). He argues later that in the study of Christianity complete objectivity, meaning a strict neutrality and exclusive reliance on empirical data, would not be desirable even if it were attainable. In *A History of Christianity* he says that "truth is not attained by reason alone. The insight that is born of faith can bring illumination" (p. xxi). Only a Christian commitment "opens the mind towards the true understanding of history" (p. xxi). The proper examination of Christianity requires an empirical study in combination with the perspective of faith.

In Latourette's methodology, Christian beliefs become principles of selection, organization, and interpretation. He thought it desirable that the history of any subject, no matter how limited in time or geography, should be written, insofar as possible, from a global point of view. Over and above scholarly considerations, the universal implications of his faith compelled him to adopt such an approach.[24] The need

20. *Expansion*, I, xvii.
21. "Teacher's Confession," p. 182.
22. See *A History of Christian Missions in China* (New York, 1929), p. vii; *Expansion*, I, xvi.
23. *Expansion*, I, xvii-xviii.
24. *Beyond the Ranges*, p. 109.

to place events in the setting of universal history is particularly urgent in the study of Christianity.

> Since Christians have claimed that Christ is essential to a comprehension of the meaning of history, since the outlook of Christianity is universal in its scope, and since from the outset the ideal has been set before the followers of Jesus of winning all men to his discipleship, the historian must ask how far that understanding and that dream have been realized. His canvas, therefore, must be all mankind from the beginning to the present.[25]

The obligation acknowledged in that passage harmonizes with his objective of demonstrating the increasing world role of the faith.

Latourette's understanding of Christianity as man's response to the gospel also broadens the sweep of his historiography. In order "to trace the entire course of the stream which issued from our Lord and of its contributions to mankind,"[26] the traditional study of Western Christianity has to be transcended. More is required than an examination of the internal affairs of the institutional church and of theological trends. The emphasis has to fall on practice rather than theory, on religion rather than doctrine. Above all, attention has to be focused on man's spiritual life. The criteria he uses to measure the progress of Christianity are thus intended also to illuminate the human response to the gospel. His criteria are geographical extent, the number and strength of new movements attributable to Jesus, and the effect of Jesus on men and cultures.[27]

Latourette also took to his work interpretive principles derived from faith. Some are implicitly Christian. He shows that religion finds its most profound explanation at the level of internal spiritual factors; more ambitiously, he theorizes that the nature of culture is determined, in the last analysis,

25. *A History of Christianity*, pp. xvi-xvii.

26. "The Place of Church History in the Training of Missionaries," in *The Life of the Church*, The Madras Series (New York & London, 1939), IV, 256.

27. LeRoy Moore, Jr. describes Latourette's emphasis on the human response to the gospel as the "pietist" approach to church history. See his *"Beyond the Ranges* — The Autobiography of Kenneth Scott Latourette; a Review Article," *Hartford Quarterly*, VIII (1968), 91-92.

by religion and individual morality. The first idea appears in his explanation of the successful expansion of Christianity, the second in his study of the church in the "revolutionary age." To explain fully the unique vitality and influence of the faith as well as the larger meaning of its historical achievements, he uses an explicitly Christian principle of interpretation. Stated simply, it is the belief "that the Christian Gospel is God's supreme act on man's behalf and that the history of Christianity is the history of what God has done for man through Christ and of man's response."[28]

In practice, how does Latourette's methodology affect his church historiography? The content of his writings is predominantly empirical. To answer the historical questions raised by his study, he assembled the necessary documentary evidence, giving the "mechanical and human factors" their proper due. *Expansion*, therefore, chiefly narrates the discoverable facts of the spread of the faith. It emphasizes the processes by which Christianity advanced. Other studies follow a similar pattern. *A History of Christianity* surveys the leading events in the life of the church since the first century. *Revolutionary Age* records the activities of modern Christianity. These works present a wealth of detail: they are virtual catalogs of names, missions, congregations, societies, revivals, and the like. Latourette's selection of material was influenced by other professional aims. Wishing to be impartial and sympathetic, he paid close attention to all major branches of Christianity. An ecumenical point of view encouraged his comprehensive coverage. His emphasis is, in addition, dictated by the pragmatic intent of dealing at length with the history of modern Christianity. Again, a professional motive coincides with a personal one: the examination of missions since the nineteenth century has to give considerable space to Latourette's own theological tradition.

His plan to study and to measure the global influence of Jesus also shapes the content and organization of his work. As a result of that plan, his writings underscore the territorial and numerical gains of Christianity, its interaction with Western and non-Western cultures, the achievements of its

28. *A History of Christianity*, p. xxi.

major branches, and its ebbs and flows over the centuries. His periodization of church history and the overall organization of his writings are based on his identification of the stages of Christian advance and recession. Using his three criteria — geographical extent, inner vitality as seen in the creation of new movements, and cultural and human impact — he divides the history of Christianity into the following periods of advance and recession: the period from the time of Christ to 500 was one of initial advance; from 500 to 950 the first and greatest recession; from 950 to 1350 the second major age of advance; from 1350 to 1500 the second major recession; from 1500 to 1750 the third age of advance; from 1750 to 1815 the third major recession; from 1815 to 1914 the fourth age of advance, "the great century"; and the latest age, since 1914, one of advance and recession, "advance through storm."[29] The volumes of *Expansion* roughly correspond to that scheme of periodization; the principal sections in *A History of Christianity* correspond exactly to it. The same scheme, harmonizing with his thesis, justifies his concentration on the past four centuries of Christianity, above all, the last century and a half. It presupposes that the faith is a growing force, becoming progressively more global and influential in the modern period. More than a quarter of the pages in *A History of Christianity* discuss events since 1815; three volumes in *Expansion* cover the "great century," and one covers the years from 1914 to 1945; and the entire five volumes of *Revolutionary Age* examine the last century and a half.

As the organization of Latourette's writings supports his thesis, so does his factual emphasis. He believes that the historical record demonstrates the increasing strength of the church. The proof is this: Christianity has spread farther, has won more adherents, and has become more deeply rooted among more peoples than any other religion. In the last century and a half its inner vitality has been displayed in the flourishing of congregations and orders, mission societies, the younger churches outside Europe, eucharistic congresses, YMCA's, theological creativity, and the ecumenical move-

29. Latourette's periodization was first worked out in *The Unquenchable Light*, pp. xvi-xvii.

ment — to mention some of the movements issuing from the faith. Its modern influence on humanity has been widened and deepened by Western expansion, the missionary enterprise, the greater number of churches and believers, and by the power of its beliefs and ideals to inspire not only its own adherents but those of other faiths. In the category of "results of Christian influence," broadly defined, Latourette places antislavery movements, the League of Nations and the United Nations, democracy, socialism, the Red Cross, numerous schools and hospitals, the reduction of languages to writing, the personalities of men such as Sun Yat Sen and Gandhi, and, above all, the changed lives of millions.

The influence of Christian belief on Latourette's historiography extends from its scope, organization, and emphasis to questions of interpretation. In *Expansion* and *Revolutionary Age*, he uses in historical explanation his convictions about the nature of religion and culture. He explains the successful expansion of Christianity as a Christian historian. In his view two of the most extraordinary periods of Christian advance were the first three centuries A.D., which witnessed the initial spread and triumph of the faith, and the nineteenth century, the "great century" of missionary success. As a diligent historian, he details the peculiar features of both periods that help to account for the expansion of Christianity. In the case of the early Christian centuries, he points to the conditions in the Roman Empire favorable to the spread of a new religion, noting the empire's unity, its relative tolerance of religious differences, and the widespread search for spiritual certainties. Christianity was specifically benefited by the presence of religious and moral ideas that anticipated its own. Above all, the endorsement of Constantine was crucial (*Expansion*, I, 6-44, 163). With similar care, he cites the circumstances in the nineteenth century that facilitated the missionary enterprise. Among them were the wealth made available by the Industrial Revolution, new means of transportation and communication, the atmosphere of optimism and self-confidence, and especially the overseas expansion of Europeans and the resultant breakdown of some non-European cultures (IV, 18-20).

Although Latourette takes into account the historical background of these two periods of Christian advance, he says in *Expansion* that

> in the last analysis the spread of a faith depends not only upon externally congenial circumstances, but upon inward vitality, something in the nature of the religion or sect which commands such enthusiastic devotion that it impels its adherents to propagate it. No matter how favourable the environment, where this inward dynamic is wanting no expansion takes place (II, 14).

It is a "plain matter of history," he writes, that the "vitality of . . . Christianity, when traced back to its source, has its origin primarily in the impulse which came from Jesus" (I, 168-169). The "impulse from Jesus" he defines as the belief in his "life, character, teachings, deeds, death, and resurrection" and the experience of moral and spiritual rebirth through him (I, 60; 167-168). So the main dynamic of Christianity comes from Jesus and beliefs about him. The "impulse from Jesus" was the underlying cause of the characteristics that made the early church attractive to the Roman world, from its superior organization to its moral and spiritual witness (I, 164-167). By the same token, it was responsible for the vitality, displayed particularly in evangelical Protestantism, that carried forward the religious and humanitarian work of nineteenth-century missions (IV, 45-46).

As a causal factor, the "impulse from Jesus" is sufficiently elastic to serve both an historical and a supernatural explanation of Christian vigor and expansion. Though Latourette's emphasis upon that factor is perhaps compatible with secular scholarship, it accords the inner life an unusual degree of primacy and autonomy. In effect, it gives his treatment Christian overtones.

Those overtones are even more pronounced in his interpretation of the "revolutionary age," the period since the Enlightenment. More sweeping and conjectural than his explanation of Christian expansion, that interpretation not only highlights religious factors but also views events in moralistic terms. In *Expansion* he underscores the role of personal religious experience to account for the successes of the faith;

in *Revolutionary Age* he suggests that the cultural influence of Christianity and the moral conduct of individuals were central to understanding modern history. His general interpretation of events since the eighteenth century grows out of the attempt to clarify a "seeming paradox" of the period, that is, the extraordinary vitality and unprecedented expansion and influence of Christianity on the one side and the rise of threats to the church as grave as it had known on the other. His understanding of the revolutionary age provides the setting for a detailed examination of world Christianity intended to show its staying power and continued vigor despite threats and setbacks, indeed its ability to find in adversity opportunities for new advances and achievements.

Latourette's interpretation of the revolutionary age and the "seeming paradox" of the age converge at two important points.[30] First, the forces that defined the period also identified the threats to the faith. Second, the menacing features of the past few centuries to a greater or lesser degree had their source in Christianity and Western Christendom. The aspects of the revolution that he singles out include industrialization, urbanization, science, scholarship, democracy, nationalism, socialism, communism, and secular intellectual traditions. Although many of these phenomena had conferred benefits on mankind, they also challenged the faith in the forms, for example, of social injustice, the atomization of society, alternate views of man and life, the study of comparative religion and biblical criticism, the secular state, materialism, militant atheism, and religious skepticism and unbelief. Together they threatened Christianity by contributing to the formation of a secular civilization. The revolutionary age became increasingly secular and self-confident. Spurred by expanding knowledge and technologies, modern culture adopted as its chief aim the creation of the "good life" here and now through economic modernization. At the same time, it rendered obsolete traditional social functions of religion and dulled awareness of the supernatural. In many ways it was either indifferent or hostile to religion. The forces

30. Latourette's interpretation is found primarily in *Revolutionary Age*, I, ch. 5; IV, ch. 1.

shaping the revolutionary centuries exploded in wars and revolutions directly damaging the faith. In general, the threats and explosions of the age intensified after the eighteenth century and became worldwide in the twentieth.

Although Latourette proposes a causal relationship between them in *Revolutionary Age,* he does not think that the revolutionary age and the threats to religion were simply the by-products of Christianity and Western Christendom. They were "caricatures or perversions of the Gospel," representing "man's misuse of what came through Jesus" (I, 27; 121). Individuals exercising their freedom of choice were blameworthy for social injustice, secularism, wars, and communism. Christians and non-Christians alike shared responsibility for creating dangers to the faith; through mixed purposes, both had misused "God's good gifts" (V, 533). Yet Latourette indicates that the worst distortions of Christianity, the most serious challenges to the church, came from unbelievers, like Marx and Engels, who deliberately attacked religion (V, 530-531).

The menace to Christianity was only one side of the revolutionary age. The other, and more significant side, was the unprecedented advance of the faith. Taken together, the themes of challenge and advance resulted in a general interpretation of modern history. It found in the cultural influence of Christianity the main shaping factor of the modern world, the source of both good and evil, depending on man's right or wrong use of "what came through Jesus." The double movement of the right use of "God's good gifts" versus their wrong use explains for Latourette the apparent paradox of the church in the revolutionary age. Because of man's contradictory behavior, good fruits and perversions of the gospel existed side by side. Even so, Latourette's optimistic thesis remains essentially intact. With perhaps evangelical Protestantism uppermost in mind, he holds that in spite of the setbacks and continuing threats to the faith, movements issuing from Christianity "enabled millions of individuals to live triumphantly in the midst of revolution and, inspired and empowered by him [Jesus], to devise and use means to offset the destruction and to make the revolutions contribute to the welfare of great segments of mankind and, indeed, of all the human race" (I, 121).

Latourette's discussions of Christian expansion and the revolutionary age illustrate how he combines secular and religious assumptions in historical analysis. His explanations incorporate an emphasis on spiritual and moral factors and, in the case of his treatment of the revolutionary age, even some unmistakable judgments of faith. They mark the movement in his work from implicit to explicit Christian interpretation. In the main body of his studies, he remains the secular historian in most of his discourse, rarely speaking as a believer. Consistent with his sense of professionalism, he generally reserved statements of faith for prefaces, introductory chapters, and especially chapters of summation, thus the last chapters in *Expansion, A History of Christianity,* and *Revolutionary Age.* He also expands on those statements in auxiliary works of interpretation written from an outspoken Christian point of view.[31] In concluding chapters and apologetic writings, he answers as a man of faith the historical and theological questions raised by his study. In those places, he attempts to show how religious truth must supplement historical analysis and how the course of events tends to confirm Christian belief. There he also completes his task by reaffirming a Christian understanding of history.

At the conclusion of his church histories, Latourette makes it clear that historical explanation, even if it stresses religious and moral factors, cannot fully account for the successful expansion of Christianity, the paradox of the modern church, and the fact that the life of Jesus has been the most influential ever lived and that its effect has continued to mount. These phenomena have to be seen from a Christian perspective. The advances of the faith and the worldwide influence of Jesus can be explained by the same biblical assertion: God is at work in Christ judging and reconciling men to

31. See *Anno Domini: Jesus, History and God* (New York, 1940) and *The Unquenchable Light,* which complemented *Expansion. Christianity Through the Ages* summarizes his life's work from a Christian point of view. His observations on the meaning of history are developed most fully in *What I Believe,* and particularly "Christian Understanding."

himself.[32] At the end of *Revolutionary Age,* Latourette spells
out his religious explanation of the paradox of Christianity
that he had hinted at earlier: in accordance with the parable
of Jesus, the wheat and the weeds must grow together in the
same field, so that the "chronic ills and evils of mankind" and
"the forces issuing from the love of God in Christ" are both
increasing at the same time (V, 534). Human error and im-
morality are "to be expected from the measure of free will
God has given to man in His desire to beget sons and not to
create robots" (V, 533).

In following these implications through his historical
explanation, Latourette also deals with the theological riddles
of history's meaning, the uniqueness of Jesus' mission, and
the success of God's purposes in time. Not appealing to faith
alone, he proposes that historical research seems to support
orthodox solutions to those riddles. At the end of *Revolutionary
Age* the question "What if anything is the meaning of the
story we have endeavoured to narrate and in this chapter to
summarize?" is answered by the words, "May we say at once
that much seems strangely to fit into what Christians have
believed about the universe, mankind, God, and the fashion
in which God works?" (V, 531). Largely on the basis of evidence gathered in defense of his thesis, he declares more
confidently that "the course of history has confirmed" St.
Paul's insight when he "saw in the cross both the power of
God and the wisdom of God" (V, 532). In the penultimate
chapter of *Expansion,* he writes: "'In him was life and the
life was the light of man.' In the first century that had been
an assertion of faith. By the twentieth century experience had
made it demonstrated fact" (VII, 482).

Latourette's efforts to reconcile faith and history culmi-
nate in a Christian interpretation of history. Although he
characterizes his understanding as an unadorned biblical
view, based upon faith, he feels that it was substantiated to a
considerable degree by the record of human experience. An
examination of the New Testament upheld, he believed, the
historicity of the central articles of faith, such as those assert-

32. *Expansion,* VII, 504; *Anno Domini,* p. 9.

ing the virgin birth and the bodily resurrection of Jesus.[33]
He does not, however, develop this argument. The burden
of his case for the verification of Christianity rests not on the
historical Jesus but on the evidence of his transforming influence over the centuries. In any event, his beliefs come
close to forming a natural theology, with history taking the
place of nature.

Thus Latourette's overview of events consists of biblical
affirmations closely related to historiography. It declares that
man, created in God's image, is free to obey or disobey the
law of love. Judgment manifests itself in the personal and
social tragedies that result from his disregard of that law.
Judgment reaches a climax in war. But in Latourette's theology, as in his studies, God's pursuit of man, not the tragic
nature of history, is the major theme.

> The course of history is God's search for man. God is
> judge, but He judges that He may save him and trans-
> form him. God's grace, the love which man does not
> deserve and cannot earn, respects man's free will and
> endeavors to reach man through the incarnation, the
> cross, and the Holy Spirit.[34]

On the basis of observable evidence, Latourette asserts
that God's redemptive purpose makes progress with the passing of time. The reality of salvation is apparent in individual
lives and in the activities of the church. Moreover, "from the
Churches there have come, never more than in the past
century and a half, impulses and movements 'for the healing
of the nations.' These I believe to be the work of God the
Holy Spirit." Thus, according to this view, the beneficial
results of Christianity that Latourette often cites are actually
divinely inspired. Although the redemption traceable to
Christ "is increasingly potent," the Kingdom of God cannot
be brought to completion within history.[35] As the nature of
the revolutionary age indicates, both good and evil exist until
the consummation of time. "Beyond history . . . God is 'to

33. See *A History of Christianity*, pp. 34-35, 58, 60; *Beyond the Ranges*,
pp. 73-74.
34. "Christian Understanding," p. 265.
35. *What I Believe*, pp. 54-55.

gather all things in one in Christ, which are in heaven and which are on earth.' God has always been sovereign, and in the cross and resurrection He signally triumphed, but beyond history His sovereignty is to be seen as complete."[36] In this passage Latourette reveals his hope that God's love will eventually embrace all men.[37] Though perhaps at odds with his orthodox background, his universalism is a fitting extension of his optimistic thought.

In the preceding pages we have seen how Latourette tried to reconcile his two careers and commitments. His task was obviously facilitated by the nature of ecclesiastical studies. He was a serious practitioner of straight academic history; yet, within the framework of secular scholarship, he defined his overall purpose in a religious fashion, allowed private beliefs to influence his methodology, and at important points in explanation emphasized spiritual and moral factors. Stepping outside that framework, he introduced explicit Christian interpretation. On the whole, the function of religious presuppositions in his work is to guide, serve, and supplement, but not to supplant, the empirical study of the past. In this manner his works achieve a partial synthesis of theology and conventional history.

How well does Latourette reconcile faith and history? Let us briefly consider both sides of the question. On the negative side, religious beliefs are sometimes destructive of the "good" history to which he aspires. In certain instances they interfere with proper objectivity, balance, and analysis. He is too partial to the church when he ignores the spiritual and cultural arrogance underlying the missionary enterprise and when he plays down the damage missions have done to foreign societies. Rather uncritically, he selects and interprets data in a way designed to underscore the vitality and influence of Christianity. Furthermore, despite his effort at fair coverage, he still highlights the achievements of Protestant missions. In trying to show the human response to the gospel, the quality of Christian spiritual life, he pursues an elusive goal. Lacking necessary biographical information, he

36. "Christian Understanding," p. 266.
37. Cf. *What I Believe*, p. 56; *Christianity Through the Ages*, p. 22.

falls back on the less than satisfactory method of counting converts, listing new religious organizations, and speculating on the cultural impact of the faith. In his explication of the threats to modern Christianity, he subordinates analysis to moral judgments. Is secularization primarily the result of wrong-headed personal decisions or is it primarily the consequence of the Western cultural heritage and of a more complex society in formation? In any case, although he may rightly have insisted on individual responsibility, his primary obligation as historian is to show the conditioned nature of human actions.

Finally, the optimistic terms of Latourette's identification of universal church history with salvation history call into question both his historical perception and his theological understanding. Can the dividing line between good and evil be as sharply drawn as it is in his history and theology? Is a Christian interpretation of history best confirmed by an expansionist view of the faith? Is the history of the church really such a success story? Can missionary gains and greater church unity compensate for the secularization of culture, the losses caused by Communism, and the social malaise of modern industrial society? In a word, Latourette has constructed an inadequate interpretive framework. Understandably, it has found no fervent followers.

These and other flaws should not obscure the creative role of Christian experience and assumptions in Latourette's work. His scholarly dedication and achievement can be attributed in some measure to a religious conception of the historian's task. Personal sympathies and convictions help to explain his pioneering research and publications. Moreover, his theological position encouraged a revisionist methodology that challenged parochialism in church studies and encouraged a revisionist interpretation that questioned one-sided pessimism. Partly as a result of his contribution, no serious survey of modern Christianity can now overlook churches outside Europe and North America. And no balanced study of the nineteenth century can ignore evidence of Christianity's vitality. Guided by faith, he has also supplemented an empirical, external view of church history with a religious, inside view. In so doing, he has raised a legitimate question: Is a naturalistic conception of religion satisfactory? In this connection, he has made a distinctive contribution by reminding a secular and scientifically minded age of a spiritual interpretation of life. Whatever its shortcomings, the apologetic side of his work may still possess merit for many believers. After all, he upheld orthodoxy and related it to historical study. In short, he continued the tradition of the Christian historian.

What can be said, then, about the attempt to reconcile faith and history? On balance, Latourette demonstrates that in the hands of an accomplished scholar, a Christian point of view need not, any more than some other point of view, undermine a serious investigation of the past. At worst, the assumptions of the believer occasionally distort historical reality. At best, they inspire the search for truth and even have heuristic value. In any event, they help to broaden the range of interpretation. Latourette also illustrates that the Christian historian, as a conscientious professional, need not adopt a position of moral and theological neutrality: not only in ecclesiastical studies but also in cultural, philosophical, and general history, he has opportunities for expressing personal values and insights. And nothing prevents him from acting as a Christian spokesman in writings set apart from technical studies, notably social criticism and theology of history. As we have seen in Latourette's case, less easily resolved is the problem of reinterpreting history in the light of Christian revelation. That remains the Christian historian's most vexing single assignment.

Dooyeweerd as Historian[1]

DALE K. VAN KLEY

THE SO-CALLED PHILOSOPHY of the idea of law, developed by professors Herman Dooyeweerd and Dirk Hendrik Vollenhoven at the Free University of Amsterdam during the last several decades, has long enjoyed and continues to exert a limited but important influence among Calvinist Christians in North America. Its most articulate spokespersons are now concentrated in the Association for the Advancement of Christian Scholarship at Toronto, but it has scattered and vocal representatives in many other areas. Recently — especially at the close of the last decade and the beginning of this — it began to shake off its associations with the country of its origin and win a considerable following among American college students in some Reformed and evangelical institutions, partly, I suspect, because of the coincidence of some of its emphases with those of the radical new left. Apart from whatever intrinsic merits it might possess, therefore, the philosophy of the idea of law deserves some serious attention and close scrutiny because of its influence alone.

1. Since this paper's original presentation to a Calvin College History Department colloquium in April 1972, and shortly after its final preparation for publication, two articles have appeared on precisely the same subject: Nick Van Til, "Dooyeweerd's 'History' and the Historian," *Pro Rege* [a quarterly faculty publication of Dordt College], II (Dec. 1973), 7-15; and Earl W. Kennedy, "Herman Dooyeweerd on History: An Attempt to Understand Him," *Fides et Historia*, IV, 1 (Fall 1973), 1-21. As the title suggests, Kennedy's article consists mainly in an attempt to explain Dooyeweerd's thought on the subject of history and, except for the last two pages, is not critical. Van Til's article, in contrast, is quite critical; but I fear that readers not already acquainted with Dooyeweerd's system will find it a bit opaque. For those able to understand it, however, the article contains some highly incisive criticisms: in particular, I found Van Til's few comments about Dooyeweerd's definition of history very helpful in clarifying my own thought on this subject, and his unfortunately brief remarks about the implication of Dooyeweerd's time-eternity dualism for the "miraculous" in

The philosophy of the idea of law is a closed, meticulously elaborated, and architectonic philosophical system that claims to explain both theoretical and nontheoretical human experience. It claims to be a uniquely Christian philosophy, faithfully constructed according to biblical directives. Now it is not my intention to examine either of these claims, at least in a direct and forthright fashion. To do so would entail my functioning as both philosopher and theologian, and I make no pretensions about being either. What especially interests me, rather, is a third claim this philosophy makes about itself, namely to provide indispensable directives by which to undertake any of the various academic disciplines in a radically Christian way. To be more specific, I would like to examine the applicability of this claim to one of these disciplines in particular, the writing of history. In other words, as a professional historian, I would like to explore what seem to be some of the implications, both explicit and implicit, of the Dooyeweerdian system for the writing of history, and to subject these to some critical reflection. It goes without saying, however, that to the extent that I might find the philosophy of the idea of the law wanting in its ability to adequately make sense out of past human experience, I would also regard its other claims — to best account for human experience as a whole and to be uniquely Christian — as only precariously founded.

The Dooyeweerdian insistence that history should be written in a distinctively Christian way quite logically implies one assumption — common among American historians at least since Carl Becker and Charles Beard — that value-oriented histories are not only possible but indeed inevitable, and that a neutral or "objective" kind of history upon which all historians could agree does not exist.[2] That such is Dooye-

---

history I found most intriguing. My own paper, in any case, attempts to be both explanatory and critical, and I therefore trust that a legitimate place yet exists for it in the burgeoning bibliography on the subject.

2. Carl L. Becker, "Everyman His Own Historian," *American Historical Review*, XXXVII (Jan. 1932), 221-236; Charles A. Beard, "Written History as an Act of Faith," *American Historical Review*, XXXIX (Jan. 1934), 219-229.

weerd's meaning is made clear by the import of his whole philosophy, which is in large measure a diatribe against what he calls the "dogma concerning the autonomy of philosophical thought" or the notion that human reason alone, unguided by any pre-theoretical assumptions or commitments, can arrive at some universally acknowledged and objective "truth," whether in history or in any other academic discipline.[3] At the same time, however, Dooyeweerd emphatically rejects a position closely associated with the acknowledgment of the subjective character of written history, namely historical relativism. In its most thoroughgoing form, historical relativism — or "historicism," as Dooyeweerd calls it — denies objective validity not only to any account of the past, but to all conceptions of truth indiscriminately, and regards all human values, ideals, and versions of truth as no more than the products of unique and irretrievable sets of historical circumstances. According to Dooyeweerd, this position errs in making the "historical viewpoint the all-encompassing one" and "ends in a spiritual nihilism," which, best exemplified by Spengler's *The Decline of the West*, is "one of the most alarming symptoms of the beginning of a fundamental crisis of Western culture. . . ."[4]

Dooyeweerd, then, wants to steer clear of both the Scylla of the neutral, objective, or scientific conception of history and the Charybdis of thoroughgoing historical relativism. To perform this delicate maneuver, he elevates one of the myriad perspectives available to the historian — his own "Christian" philosophy — to the level of a universally valid criterion that enables the historian not only to correctly interpret the past but also to account for the variety of "apostate" interpretations competitive with his own. Now it is not at all my intention here to condemn by association, but the precise nature of Dooyeweerd's approach might be made clearer by a comparison to that of the Marxists. Neither Dooyeweerd nor the Marxists deny the value-determined nature of much, indeed all, historical writing. On the contrary, both make much of

3. Herman Dooyeweerd, *In the Twilight of Western Thought: Studies in the Pretended Autonomy of Philosophical Thought* (Philadelphia, 1960), p. 1 — hereafter cited as *Twilight*.
4. *Twilight*, pp. 62-63.

it. Again, both raise one of the available philosophical perspectives from which history can be written to the level of a universally and objectively valid criterion: Dooyeweerd elevates his own "Christian" philosophy, and the Marxists elevate Marx's dialectical materialism. Thus, both exempt themselves from what they regard as the arbitrarily subjective nature of most historical writing. And just as Dooyeweerd explains the existence of philosophical perspectives other than his own by reference to their "apostate" character, so the Marxists account for the existence of other historical viewpoints by reference to the class-determined consciousness of their authors.

Now the nature of Marxist history is well known because of the number and quality of its practitioners. For better or worse, the same cannot be said of Dooyeweerdian history, because its proponents have so far been much more prolific in philosophical directives than in concrete productions. To determine the probable character of the latter, we must unfortunately resort to speculation, and such speculation, if it is to be at all instructive, must begin with a short summary of the main tenets of the philosophy of the idea of the law.[5]

II

I mentioned above that the philosophy of the idea of law is directed primarily against the doctrine of the autonomy of theoretical thought, against the conviction that undirected theoretical or scientific "reason" is the true and sufficient starting point of all philosophical and scientific activity. Faith in this doctrine's infallibility is the one assumption that Dooyeweerd finds common to the seemingly infinite variety of philosophical viewpoints and scientific disagreements. Yet, if the doctrine of the autonomy of theoretical thought is really tenable, he asks, why is it not possible for the various philosophical schools in western Europe to arrive at some kind of consensus? Is it possible, he further asks, that the doctrine of the autonomy of theoretical thought presents only a sham unity, that it really consists in a multiplicity of possible mean-

5. This brief summary is derived primarily from Dooyeweerd's *Twilight* and *Transcendental Problems of Philosophic Thought* (Grand Rapids, 1948); it is derived secondarily from J. M. Spier, *What is Calvinistic Philosophy?* (Grand Rapids, 1953), and Ronald H. Nash, *Dooyeweerd and the Amsterdam Philosophy* (Grand Rapids, 1962).

ings, and that it conceals rather than reveals the true starting points of philosophical and scientific inquiry, which might consist of presuppositions of a wholly different character? He concludes that the state of philosophical affairs in western Europe, if not sufficient by itself to justify such a suspicion, at least warrants an attempt to subject the doctrine of the autonomy of theoretical thought to thoroughgoing scrutiny, or what he calls a "transcendental critique."[6]

When Dooyeweerd further asks what characterizes theoretical or scientific thought, he finds that it consists in an antithetical relationship that pits the logical aspect of our thought against the non-logical aspects of human experience. This way of stating the matter already anticipates his most important conclusions. Manifestly, he does not consider the antithetical structure of theoretical thought to be at all representative of "reality." In other words, it is illicit to substitute the terms "self" or "knowing subject" in the place of "the logical aspect of our thought," and the terms "reality" or "empirical reality" for "the non-logical aspects of human experience." To do so would be to make theoretical thought the essence of the human self, or, in other words, to assume the very doctrine of the autonomy of theoretical thought which it is his purpose to examine. In ordinary experience, Dooyeweerd insists, the human self or subject is not at all pitted in an antithetical way against its object, empirical reality, but rather the two go hand in hand, as it were, in a harmonious relationship. Were it otherwise, he contends, knowledge itself would be quite impossible. The theoretical attitude of thought he regards as a highly artificial mental posture in which the logical aspect of our thought, to state the matter another way, dissociates itself from the other aspects of human experience and attempts to subsume these under some logical concept. The implication is already clear that the logical aspect of our thought is only one of many aspects of human experience and cannot be arbitrarily identified with the ultimate unity of the human self.[7]

6. *Twilight*, pp. 1-6.
7. *Transcendental Problems of Philosophic Thought*, pp. 29-33—hereafter cited as *Transcendental Problems*.

This is perhaps the place to enlarge on these various aspects of human experience, which together constitute the most well-known feature of the Dooyeweerdian system. Dooyeweerd lists fifteen such aspects. They are, in ascending order, the numerical, spatial, physical, kinetic, biotic, sensory, logical, historical, linguistic, social, economic, aesthetic, juridical, moral, and pistical. These aspects, or "modalities," are not, of course, to be identified with empirical reality itself but are rather to be understood as ways or modes in which we experience empirical reality.[8] The scale of modal aspects of our experience, Dooyeweerd says, "makes sense only within the order of time. It refers to a supra-temporal, central unity and fulness of meaning in our experiential world, which is refracted in the order of time, into a rich diversity of modi, or modalities of meaning, just as sunlight is refracted by a prism in a rich diversity of colors."[9] (I quote this passage partly because it is one of the few instances I can recall in which Dooyeweerd has recourse to a metaphor.) The various modalities are hierarchically structured in the order I have listed them so that all except the base modality (the numerical) are founded on those preceding them in the scale. And although Dooyeweerd insists that the special meaning of each aspect is irreducible to any other (Dooyeweerd calls this meaning the "modal kernel"), the various modalities are mutually coherent and interrelated in such a way that the full meaning of each aspect "recalls" those preceding it in the scale ("retrospective moments") and "anticipates" those following it in the scale ("anticipatory moments"). Thus the meaning of any aspect is at once irreducible and fixed when considered by itself, and ambiguous, or "multivocal," when considered in relation to the others.[10]

In what Dooyeweerd variously calls "pre-scientific," "pre-theoretical," and "naive" experience (I take it he means ordinary, day-to-day experience), we do not distinguish among these modalities or concentrate on one to the exclusion of the others. Rather, we experience concrete things (buildings,

8. *Twilight,* pp. 6-7; *Transcendental Problems,* p. 41.
9. *Twilight,* p. 7.
10. *Twilight,* pp. 9-11; *Transcendental Problems,* pp. 42-48.

trees, animals, people, etc.) which function, in our consciousness, in all the aspects of our "temporal experiential horizon." Thus, for example, water obviously functions in relation
to knowing subjects in a numerical, spatial, physical, kinetic,
and sensory way, but when used in the sacrament of baptism
functions even in a pistical or fideistic fashion. And though
all empirical entities function in all the aspects of our "temporal experiential horizon," each individual entity or structure is specially characterized or "qualified" by one of these
aspects ("typical structures of individuality and totality"), in
a manner reminiscent of the way in which Leibnitz's "dominant monad" gives identity to a whole conglomeration of
monads. Thus a cathedral is specially characterized or qualified by its faith or pistical aspect, although it obviously functions in all the others. It is important for Dooyeweerd to
insist that in "naive" or "pre-theoretical" experience we encounter no antithetical relation between ourselves and empirical reality. Without hesitation we ascribe objective functions to inanimate things, such as ascribing to water the
ability to sustain life, even though we know full well that
water is an inanimate substance that cannot function as a
subject. Naive experience is therefore characterized by an
harmonious subject-object relationship, which is very different from the antithetical nature of theoretical thought. Dooyeweerd further maintains that ordinary experience is not
itself a theory of reality, but rather the ultimate test of any
such theory; it is a fundamental datum of human experience,
which any philosophical system must satisfactorily account
for on pain of being "erroneous in its fundamentals."[11]

To return, now, to the antithetical nature of theoretical
thought, in which the logical function of our thought artificially separates itself from the non-logical aspects of experience
and seeks to comprehend these in a logical concept. Theoretical thought must surpass this antithetical character by attempting a "synthesis between the logical and non-logical
aspects if a logical concept of the non-logical modes is to be
possible."[12] But no sooner is this attempt made, Dooyeweerd

11. *Twilight,* pp. 13-18; *Transcendental Problems,* pp. 41-42.
12. *Twilight,* p. 18.

contends, than a fundamental problem emerges. What is the central starting point from which this theoretical synthesis can proceed? At this point the adherents to the dogma of the autonomy of theoretical thought (that is, those who maintain that theoretical thought itself provides this central starting point) are caught on the horns of an embarrassing dilemma, for there is nothing within theoretical thought itself that justifies choosing either the logical aspect or any of the nonlogical aspects of our experience (in other words, either of the poles of the antithetical structure of theoretical thought itself) as the proper synthetical point of departure. The fundamental diversity inherent in theoretical thought itself prevents those who wish to regard it as the true synthetical starting point from reducing this diversity into any kind of synthetical unity. Yet this is precisely what they are obliged to do, with the unhappy result that they illicitly absolutize one or another of the many (in fact) irreducible aspects of our experience. This illicit operation Dooyeweerd regards as the origin of the many mutually exclusive "isms" that have bedeviled the history of Western thought: behaviorism, historicism, and such like. All have at least this in common, that they attempt to reduce the rich and fundamental diversity of our experience to one of its many aspects.[13]

By now Dooyeweerd thinks he has demonstrated the futility of theoretical thought's attempt to locate its true starting point from within itself. The existence of so many "isms" or absolutizations of various experiential aspects, which find no real justification within theoretical thought, themselves point rather to the operation of certain nontheoretical motives that "seem to be masked," Dooyeweerd says, "by the dogma concerning the autonomy of philosophical thought."[14] Hence, theoretical thought is eventually forced outside itself in its search for the unified human selfhood or ego, where the intrinsic diversity of theoretical thought finds its ultimate unity and origin. But here again another "transcendental" problem rears its ugly head: how can theoretical thought possibly put its finger on the essential character of this human self or ego?

13. *Twilight*, pp. 18-22; *Transcendental Problems*, pp. 37-40.
14. *Twilight*, p. 3.

Its every attempt to do so seems condemned in advance to the illicit absolutization of one of the various ways in which this human selfhood functions: a logical "I," an historical "I," a psycho-physical "I," and so forth. The unified human self-hood is indeed the very condition of theoretical thought as well as "naive" experience, but its position as such seems to render it forever inaccessible to logical definition. Everyone will recognize here the problem Kant attempted to solve in the *Critique of Pure Reason*. Dooyeweerd admires Kant for his efforts but argues that he ultimately erred in identifying the human self with its logical function, or, in other words, with theoretical thought itself.[15]

Philosophical thought, then, finally returns empty-handed from its long search for humanity. Dooyeweerd somewhat abruptly concludes at this point that the true nature of the human selfhood can be understood not in relation to our "temporal experiential horizon," nor even in relation to other human selves (personalism), but only in relation to its divine origin. This is as much as saying that it can only be understood by having recourse to revelation. Dooyeweerd admits that this is to go beyond philosophy, but his argument seems to be that only by means of divine revelation can we make any sense out of human experience. What divine revelation reveals, according to Dooyeweerd, is that the human center or heart lies beyond its "temporal experiential horizon" — in other words, beyond time itself — and that it is the repository of the image of God. Considered by itself, in relation to other selves or in relation to creation, the human heart remains a vacuous concept. It is only in relation to its divine origin that it acquires a positive content. This relation can be of two sorts — correct or apostate. The correct relation to God, in which we recognize ourselves as his fallen creatures in need of redemption, will in turn properly orient us in our relations to our fellow man (the second table of the law) and our "temporal experiential horizon" (the cultural mandate). An apostate relation to God — it is still a relationship to God, Dooyeweerd insists — results in an attempt to find ultimate meaning within the created order itself, which in turn gives

15. *Twilight*, pp. 21-26; *Transcendental Problems*, pp. 49-52.

rise to notions like the "pretended autonomy of philosophical thought," together with the inevitable "isms" in their train.[16]

The relationship between the self's center or heart and its divine origin is in all events of a religious character, and Dooyeweerd calls it the "religious basic motive" (sometimes translated "ground motive"). It is within these "religious basic motives," whether of a correct or an apostate character, that Dooyeweerd finally locates the true starting points of philosophical inquiry, and which the doctrine of the autonomy of philosophical thought serves only to conceal. The correct or Christian religious basic motive Dooyeweerd calls the motive of creation-fall-redemption, which "should not be confounded with the ecclesiastical articles of faith, which refer to this motive." "The radical sense [of creation-fall-redemption] can only be explained by the Holy Spirit, operating in the heart, or the religious center of our consciousness, within the communion of the invisible Catholic Church." Moreover, this "basic religious motive" uncovers the "real root, or center, of human nature and unmasks the idols of the human ego, which arise by seeking this center within the temporal horizon of our experience with its modal diversity of aspects."[17]

Apostate religious basic motives, on the other hand, would seem to be as numerous as the ways in which the self might attempt to locate itself and its true origin within this "temporal horizon of experience." Nonetheless, Dooyeweerd distinguishes three apostate religious basic motives which, he thinks, have successively dominated the culture of western Europe. The first is the form-matter motive of classical Greek thought, itself the result of a combination of the Greeks' private animistic religion and the public religion of the Olympian deities. It deifies both the inexorable "process of birth and decline," or the biotic aspect of our experience (matter), and measure and harmony, or the cultural aspects of our experience (form), and it pits the one against the other. The second, the medieval grace-nature motive, represents an attempted accommodation or "synthesis" between the radical biblical creation-fall-redemption motive and the Greek view of reality

16. *Twilight*, pp. 27-38; *Transcendental Problems*, pp. 49-55.
17. *Twilight*, p. 42.

as form and matter as constituting a purely natural realm (nature) containing truths accessible to unaided human reason, which is in turn dependent on divine revelation for truths concerning a complementary supernatural realm, that of grace. The final apostate religious basic motive, the modern freedom-nature motive, arose during the Italian Renaissance of the fourteenth and fifteenth centuries, when it manifested itself primarily in the form of the cult or deification of the free, autonomous human personality (freedom), which created the world and God in its own image. But that image, a mechanistic nature presided over by a God-Geometrician, in the long run ironically left no room for human freedom, which then revolted by deifying the ethical aspect of our experience in the thought of Rousseau and Kant. According to Dooyeweerd, modern humanistic thought has since oscillated between the poles of nature and freedom, up to the recent triumph of "nature" in the form of the deterministic outlook of historicism.[18]

These four religious basic motives, the creation-fall-redemption motive and the three apostate ones, have manifested themselves and must necessarily manifest themselves both in the form of articulated faiths or common beliefs (that is, through the "faith aspect" of our "temporal experiential horizon") and in the historical formation of human society (in other words, through the "historico-cultural aspect" of our "temporal experiential horizon"). The former manifestation is the object of theological investigation, the latter the object of historical research.[19]

III

So at long last and with considerable relief I return to the subject of history. But aside from the rather cryptic hint that history should have something to do with the societal manifestation of "religious basic motives" (whatever this might concretely mean), what does this philosophical system have to do with the writing of history? On the surface of it,

18. *Twilight,* pp. 39-52, 62-82; *Transcendental Problems,* pp. 59-77.
19. *Twilight,* p. 34.

little enough. To be sure, the historian notes with satisfaction
that the study of the "historical aspect" of reality finds a place
in Dooyeweerd's hierarchical scale of things, observes with
even greater satisfaction that his activities apparently rank
above those of logicians, psychologists, biologists, and even
physicists and mathematicians, but discovers with disbelief
that they rank below those of linguists, sociologists, economists, aesthetes, political scientists, and the like. More seriously, the system contains quite obvious if controversial directives for the writings of histories of Western philosophy.
But after enjoying a brief vogue associated with the name of
Arthur O. Lovejoy, the field of disembodied intellectual history has been pretty much abandoned by historians and left
to the ravages of philosophers. Professor Vollenhoven has in
fact written a Dooyeweerdian history of ancient philosophy,
which may be easily consulted by anyone sufficiently interested in that kind of exercise.[20]

But what about the collapse of the Roman Empire, the
development of feudalism, the formation of nation-states, the
French Revolution, the battle of Waterloo — events and developments, in short, usually considered "historical" and which
first come to mind when one thinks of history as an academic
discipline? In other words, what, if anything, does the philosophy of the idea of law have to say about histories of particular events, biographies of historically significant individuals, analyses of the behavior of past social groups, the study
of economic transformations — the kinds of histories that
historians generally write these days?

Perhaps Dooyeweerd's definition of history will further
enlighten us. Dooyeweerd rejects, first of all, the popular
conception of history as "all that happened in the past." Such
a conception will do very well for "naive experience," he says,
but will not do at all for history understood in a scientific,
academic sense, which, as an exercise in theoretical thought,
distinguishes the historical aspect of past events from their
other aspects and considers these events uniquely from the
historical point of view. To say it in another way, past phe-

20. Vollenhoven, *Geschiedenis der wijsbegeerte* (Franecker, 1950-?).

nomena no less than present phenomena function in all the
aspects of our experience, but when we function as historians
we artificially exclude from our consideration all aspects
of our experience of past phenomena except the historical one.
And just as entities and structures are "typified" or "qualified" by one or another of the various aspects in which they
function, so past events and phenomena, according to Dooyeweerd, are typified by one or another of these aspects, among
them the "historical" aspect, although they function in all the
others as well. Dooyeweerd lists the invention of printing and
the battle of Waterloo as typically "historical" past events
(how the battle of Waterloo also functioned, say, aesthet-
ically, juridically, ethically, and fideistically I leave to the
speculation of others); the efforts of the peasants to save their
crops on the fields of the battle of Waterloo he lists as a "non-
historical" past event, although possessed, like any other, of
an "historical" aspect.[21]

To the uninitiate the "historical" aspect of a past event
might sound a bit circular, but Dooyeweerd attaches a special meaning to the word "historical." He finds the "modal
kernel" of the "historical aspect of our experience" to consist
in "cultural formation," or man's "formative power over the
world and over its societal life." By "cultural," in turn, Dooyeweerd seems to mean the ways in which men give order to
their collective existence (the organization of the economy,
the formation of institutions such as the state, church, university, etc.), as well as the ways by which they assert control
over nature (the development of the various sciences and
arts). Further, the historical mode of experience is founded
at least indirectly on the biological aspect; hence the historical
aspect recalls, or in a sense mirrors, the "modal kernel" of the
biological aspect, which is that of growth or development.
But within the context of the historical aspect the notion of
growth or development is no longer to be understood in its
properly biological sense, but rather as the kind of develop-

21. *Twilight,* pp. 83-86, 95; Dooyeweerd, *A New Critique of Theoretical Thought,* tr. David H. Freeman, H. De Jongsta (Amsterdam
and Philadelphia, 1955), II, pp. 192-194—hereafter cited as *New
Critique.* All references will be to the second volume, which contains
the chapters on the historical "meaning-aspect."

ment over which human beings exercise a degree of control (the mistake of historicism, Dooyeweerd thinks, is that it holds to the purely biological sense of development within the historical mode of our experience, and hence conceives of historical development as determined and inevitable). For Dooyeweerd, then, history means "the cultural development of mankind"; the task of the historian is presumably to trace this development.[22]

There is in truth more to Dooyeweerd's conception of history than this, but we now possess enough of it to reassure ourselves that Dooyeweerd at least has room in his scheme of things for political history, economic history, social history, art history — in short, most any kind of history that historians write. All of these quite obviously have to do with the cultural development of mankind. But at this point an obnoxious but inevitable question presents itself: how is Dooyeweerd to account for these various kinds of history? Political history, economic history, social history and art history seem to concern the juridical, economic, social and aesthetic aspects of past human experience respectively. Now if historians are to limit themselves solely to the "historical" aspects of past human experience, are these histories illegitimate? Or do they concern the "historical" aspect of the juridical, economic, social and aesthetic aspects of past human experience? Studies of aspects of aspects? We seem to be on the border of nonsense.

Dooyeweerd would apparently reply that these are atypical, peripheral kinds of histories concerning past human events that are typified or qualified by their juridical, economic, social and aesthetic aspects, but which nonetheless possess an "historical" aspect that can be made the object of specialized studies.[23] Typically, however, historians are concerned with typically historical events, such as the battle of Waterloo or the invention of printing. But at this point another obnoxious but irrepressible question arises: how are we to determine which past events are typified by their historical aspect and which by other aspects? It would be convenient indeed for

22. *Twilight,* pp. 86-95; *New Critique,* pp. 193-204, 216-217.
23. *New Critique,* p. 197.

the historian if events were to come down to him already labeled as typically historical or typically some other thing, so that he could rivet his attention more especially upon the former. Unfortunately, however, this does not seem to be the case. If certain events can be labeled as typically historical, it would seem that they should be immediately recognizable as such. Let us take any recent event — former President Nixon's trip to China, for example — and ask ourselves whether it is typically historical. Richard Nixon himself would naturally have no doubts about it. Before he had even left Chinese soil he was able to recognize the time he spent there as a "week that changed the world." But the value of his testimony is substantially reduced when one remembers that nearly all the actions he undertook he regarded as typically "historical," or in any event, ones which historians — or rather "History" — will "record." Many others have of course also hazarded assessments of the event's historical significance, but these assessments are notoriously at variance with each other and are all too palpably related to the political sympathies or aversions of their proponents. As to the event's real historical significance, what can one say after all, other than repeat the time-worn adage that only time can tell?

What Dooyeweerd must obviously mean by a typically historical event is what historians with less fanfare call an "important" event — important, that is, by virtue of the influence over human affairs it has subsequently exerted. The importance of the event, then, can only be tentatively assessed after the passage of a considerable period of time and definitely assessed, if even then, only at the end of time. But until the expiration of such time as might enable one to assess the significance of a given event with some degree of responsibility, what is one to do with the uncooperative thing? Typify it by reference to some other of its fifteen or so functions? In that case the typical character of an event would seem to change with time. Even with regard to events that have long ago receded into the past, I defy Dooyeweerd or anyone else to produce two historians who could perfectly agree on a list of the most important ones. Dooyeweerd himself proposes the candidacy of the invention of printing and the battle of Waterloo; but these, I confess, do not get me very far.[24] The case could easily be made that the Great Depression of 1929, typified, it would seem, by its economic aspect, has already had more important consequences than the defeat of Napoleon in 1815, which was followed by some boundary rectifications and a wholly doomed attempt to undo the work of the French Revolution. As for the invention of printing, I would say — were I absolutely forced to pronounce on the matter — that it was typified by its linguistic aspect, although it was, if Mr. McLuhan is to be trusted, the most important event before the invention of mass media.

But let us have done with such logic chopping before it hacks open a pandora's box of even spinier philosophical questions, such as "what exactly are historical events anyway?" and, whatever they are, "can Dooyeweerd treat them in the same way that he does concrete, individual entities and structures?" Let us grant Dooyeweerd the obvious, which is that historians possess no monopoly over the past, that philosophers deal with past philosophers, literary critics with past poets and novelists, art critics with past artists, political scientists with past political systems, and so forth. Yet it seems to me that what distinguishes the attention of historians from that of these others is precisely its preoccupation with the past as such. To a philosopher, the fact that Descartes was a Frenchman, lived in the seventeenth century, and witnessed the Thirty Years' War and the Fronde is only of peripheral interest, whereas to the historian, who is engaged in the first instance in an attempt to reconstruct the past, they are central. And this, indeed, is the chief flaw in Dooyeweerd's definition of history as a science: that along with the "naive" conception of history it rejects the investigation of the past as an essential part of itself. Having thus deprived the discipline of history of its traditional object — the past — Dooyeweerd is forced to provide it with another, which he locates in an "historical aspect" of all phenomena, whether past, pres-

24. *Twilight*, p. 85. In the same place Dooyeweerd mentions "the great invasion of the Allied military forces in France during the last world war." He seems to harbor the opinion that "typically historical events" are mainly military ones.

ent, or future. Now, since all phenomena are specially "qualified" by one or another of the fifteen aspects of experience, it necessarily follows that at least some of them must be "qualified" by the "historical aspect," and the resultant "typically historical events" hence form the object of historical investigation in the stricter sense. But if, as I have argued, these "typically historical events" nowhere exist in reality, or at least cannot be identified with certainty, then the historian seems condemned to study the "historical aspect" of phenomena especially "qualified" by some other aspect, and hence play a lowly second fiddle to everyone else. It also seems to follow that historians could just as legitimately concern themselves with the present and the future as with the past, so long as they restricted themselves to the "historical aspect" of these.

To avoid these absurd conclusions, it seems sufficient merely to insist on the inclusion of the human past as such in any attempt to delineate the proper boundaries of historical investigation, and hence to rehabilitate at least in part the "naive" definition of history Dooyeweerd so cavalierly discards. Dooyeweerd's profoundest reason for rejecting the past as such as an element — or at least as an essential element — in his definition of history probably has to do with his characterization of our whole "experiential horizon" as "temporal." Having made time the "prism" (to use his own metaphor) through which all of reality is refracted into its various aspects, Dooyeweerd is understandably reluctant to posit any privileged relationship between any segment of time — the past — and any single aspect of reality. But the curious character of some of the results this starting point seems to yield perhaps attests to a hidden deficiency in the starting point itself.

IV

But let us return to Dooyeweerd's definition of history as "the cultural development of mankind." One might legitimately ask why it is so important for Dooyeweerd to define history in this way. Remember, first of all, Dooyeweerd's insistence that "cultural development" is not to be understood in a biologically deterministic sense, but as a process over which human beings exercise free control. Recall, secondly, his conception of human nature as fundamentally religious in character. Remember, finally, his characterization of the "religious basic motives" that, he says, have dominated the development of Western culture, and his offhand remark that the object of historical research is to uncover the manifestation of these "religious basic motives" in the "historico-cultural" aspect of our "temporal experiential horizon."[25] In, around, and through these diverse utterances, and under the philosophical jargon, seems to reside the opinion that Christian historians ought to regard all history as ultimately religious history, and that the history of the West can in fact be accounted for exclusively in terms of the four "religious basic motives" as he has defined them.

The plausibility of this view would seem to depend in part on how precisely one understood Dooyeweerd's insistence that the central core of human nature is religious. If by "religious" Dooyeweerd means the conscious acceptance of a credal faith such as Calvinism or Catholicism, the answer must obviously be in the negative. One can easily grant that during the sixteenth century some Calvinists and some Catholics sometimes did or said certain things because they were Calvinists and Catholics. There is much evidence, for example, to support the view that the French admiral Gaspard de Coligny fought on the Calvinist side in the religious civil wars because of his religious convictions, but considerable more evidence to the effect that most other aristocratic participants in these wars supported one or another side for considerations of a wholly different character. And when French Calvinists developed contractual theories of government after the Saint Bartholomew Day's Massacre in 1672, only to become enthusiastic proponents of the monarchy after it seemed that the Protestant Henry of Navarre would next succeed to the French throne, one can reasonably conclude that the political views of French Calvinists were not so much a

25. *Twilight*, p. 34.

function of their religious convictions as of considerations of a more mundane sort.[26]

But Dooyeweerd's view that an articulate faith or religious creed is itself one among many temporal manifestations of a man's "religious" orientation would seem to exclude the possibility of equating credal faiths with his understanding of "religious." Does Dooyeweerd then mean by "religious" any world-view whatever, in the sense in which Carl Becker regarded the principles of the French Enlightenment as a kind of secular religion?[27] Even if this were his meaning, it would again not get us very far in explaining the bulk of past human behavior. To take the example of the French Enlightenment, one can easily grant that it had something to do with the outbreak and character of the French Revolution of 1789, especially when it came to such activities as drawing up the Declaration of the Rights of Man and the Citizen and writing a constitution. But even here we have to take into consideration many factors of a decidedly nonideological character. In 1792 the members of the Legislative Assembly proclaimed the republic, not so much because of an "enlightened" predisposition against the monarchy, but because their monarch, Louis XVI, had been involved in traitorous relationships with the Austrian emperor, was quite unwilling to play the role of constitutional monarch assigned to him, and had already been dethroned by an armed crowd organized by the Parisian sections.

I would like to think, rather, that by "religious" Dooyeweerd means any consideration to which a man gives his ultimate loyalty, whether it be his economic well-being, social status, prestige or renown, the preservation of a certain style of life, the domination of a race, the nation's honor, or considerations of a more ideological or religious character. This is the meaning that Calvinists have generally attached to the word, and so far as history is concerned, it permits the historian to be quite open to most any kind of evidence he might

26. See, in particular, Roland Mousnier, *L'Assassinat d'Henri IV*, no. 13 in series entitled *Trente journées qui ont fait la France* (Paris, 1964), pp. 75, 81-82.
27. Carl L. Becker, *The Heavenly City of the Eighteenth-Century Philosophers* (New Haven, 1932), *passim*.

encounter. Exceptions might be made of those instances — rather numerous, it must be confessed — when people do not seem to be masters of themselves at all, when circumstances seem to dictate a single or at most a severely limited number of possible responses. I am thinking in particular of the almost Pavlovian behavior of a Louis XVI or Nicholas II on the eve of disaster. But Christianity's well-known emphasis on man's limitations would seem to do them more than justice. In any event, Dooyeweerd appears in places to suggest this meaning for the word "religious," and his system might conceivably allow for it. An apostate response to God could easily take the form of, say, "absolutizing" the economic aspect of our experience, and this "absolutizing" could take the quite nontheoretical form we commonly observe it to do. Perhaps the system then has room for an economic motivation, as well as any number of others.

I am therefore all the more discomfited by Dooyeweerd's four "basic religious motives" and the historical role he assigns to them. It might be observed at the outset that Dooyeweerd's attempt to characterize all of Western thought in terms of the successive manifestation of these "motives" represents itself a piece of historical analysis, and that of a rather dubious character. His three "apostate religious basic motives" (the Graeco-Roman form-matter motive, the medieval synthetic grace-nature motive, and the modern freedom-nature motive) strike me offhand as wholly illegitimate extrapolations from the systems of Aristotle, Thomas Aquinas, and Immanuel Kant respectively. Even if it be granted that all three were influential thinkers of the first order, and even if their "influence" be understood only as variations on dialectical themes most clearly represented by themselves, it still seems extravagant to characterize all of Western thought by reference to these themes. One could just as well choose one of any number of abiding philosophical problems — the one versus the many, say — examine successive Western philosophers' explicit or implicit responses to this problem, and conclude from this exercise that the one versus the many is the dominant theme in Western thought. Or to take a more concrete example, Voltaire, who lived during Dooyeweerd's nature-freedom epoch, occasionally evidenced some concern about the problem of whether the human will was free or determined, but it would be extravagant to conclude that this problem was Voltaire's dominant concern, or that it ever caused him any loss of sleep.

But does Dooyeweerd also really mean to say that these four "religious basic motives" are responsible in some causal sense for all of Western culture? Does he really mean to suggest that all the various economic, social, and institutional changes that have taken place in the course of European history are solely attributable to the fact that those who brought them about were in the "grip" (the word is one of his favorites) of one or another of his "religious basic motives"?[28] If this is really his opinion, then it is hardly too harsh to say that his view of the historical landscape is hopelessly obstructed by Aristophanes' clouds, and that if, as Pascal maintained, it is necessary to abase oneself to understand mathematical and geometrical truths, Dooyeweerd must even further abase himself if he is ever to comprehend the far more elementary historical truths. I do not mean to suggest that deep-seated intellectual presuppositions or world-views of one sort or another bear no relationship to the kinds of societies men construct. Lionel Rothkrug, for example, has recently demonstrated to my satisfaction that the Cartesian world-view influenced the way some Frenchmen thought about the state, and that this Cartesian conception of the state played a role (although not, in my opinion, the decisive one) in the development of seventeenth-century absolutism.[29] But to assume, for instance, that Parisian sans-culottes stormed the Bastille in 1789 because they were in the "grip" of the freedom-nature "religious motive," or that the unlettered, unwashed barbarian chieftains hewed out the feudal system after the collapse of the Carolingian Empire because they were in the "'grip"

28. That this is indeed what Dooyeweerd wishes to say is suggested by the following: "Without faith not a single movement has ever succeeded in gaining formative power in history" (*New Critique*, p. 356).
29. Lionel Rothkrug, *Opposition to Louis Fourteenth: The Political and Social Origins of the French Enlightenment* (Princeton, 1965), esp. chs. 1 and 2.

of the grace-nature "religious motive," is too preposterous on the face of it to merit serious consideration.

Far from denying any relationship between men's religious presuppositions or world-views and societal changes, I would only insist that these connections be demonstrated rather than assumed. To follow Dooyeweerd too slavishly on the cultural role of his "religious basic motives" would be to straitjacket the historian into an apriorism of the crudest sort, to "absolutize" a highly rarefied form of human motivation, and to do gross violence to the vast bulk of human experience.

V

That Dooyeweerd ultimately assigns sole causal force in the process of cultural development to what he calls "basic religious motives" becomes clearer when we return, finally, to the remaining components of his definition of history. Recall that the historical aspect of our experience presupposes and mirrors the biotic, which in the context of the former yields the notion of formative cultural development. But Dooyeweerd further insists that the historical aspect only indirectly mirrors the biotic, and that this latter is refracted, as it were, through the logical aspect of our experience, upon which the historical aspect is immediately founded. Now all logical judgments are of a normative character: when a statement is described as illogical, a normative judgment is pronounced against that statement. Hence all aspects based on the logical aspect of our experience display a similarly normative character (that is, having to do with what ought to be), illustrated by such contrasts as linguistically right or wrong, aesthetic or unaesthetic, polite or impolite, economic or uneconomic, lawful or unlawful, moral or immoral, and believing or unbelieving. This means that historical judgments are likewise of a normative character: they determine whether a given development is "in line with or contrary to the requirements of historical development," or in other words, whether they are reactionary or progressive. If correctly pronounced, these judgments are not subjective or arbitrary, but rather conform to "an objective norm of historical development which implicitly lies at the foundation of the cultural historical mode of experience."[30]

It is evident, then, that Dooyeweerd is working with some notion of progress, or at least believes that the use of the terms "progressive" and "reactionary" in historical literature is not necessarily arbitrary and capricious. Given the continuing and — especially in the light of the more recent ecological awareness — ever more justifiable disenchantment with the idea of progress, it is always surprising to encounter anyone willing to subscribe to a notion of human progress, and so his position on this matter is intriguing indeed. Now one thing that can be said about all theories of human progress is that they are intimately related to some goal or utopia toward which history is presumably moving and in terms of which any historical development can be judged as progressive or reactionary. If — to employ an example used by Carl Becker on a similar occasion — the goal of my writing this paper is to fill thirty or forty pages with ink, it is incontestable that I have been making progress in terms of this goal simply by scribbling one sentence after another. But if, on the other hand, my readers are so perverse as to think that my goal should be to enlighten them on the subject of Dooyeweerd's conception of history, some of them might judge my performance so far as progressive, others, no doubt, as downright reactionary.[31] So what is the goal or *summum bonum* toward which Dooyeweerd's history is progressing?

To ask this question is to inquire concerning the normative content of the historical aspect. Its mere foundational dependence on the logical aspect reveals, as we have seen, that the aspect of free cultural development possesses a normative character, but nothing in the purely foundational moments in the meaning of the historical aspect (what Dooyeweerd variously calls the historical "concept" or the his-

---

30. *Twilight*, pp. 95-97. Following Dooyeweerd here, I have limited myself solely to the logical analogy of contradiction in the historical aspect. For the analogies of identity, diversity, and imputation, see *New Critique*, pp. 229-232.
31. Carl L. Becker, *Progress and Power*, Vintage edition (New York, 1965), p. 10.

torical aspect's "restricted" or "closed" meaning) reveals anything at all about the real normative content of cultural development, or, in other words, what these norms actually are.
At least among the normative aspects of our experience it
is one of the peculiarities of the historical aspect that its
normative content can be discovered only by reference to its
anticipatory or prospective moments in the transcendental
direction of time (what Dooyeweerd variously terms the historical aspect's "disclosed" or "opened-up" meaning or, again,
the historical "Idea").[32] This is as much as saying that to
uncover the norms governing historical development we must
tiredly follow Dooyeweerd up the remaining seven rungs of
his modal ladder of experience and examine what he calls
the "analogical" meaning of each of these prospective aspects
in the context of the historical aspect.

This mouthful is in turn as much as saying that cultural
development, if it is to be truly progressive, must be "opened
up" and "guided" by the normative aspects above it on the
modal scale of experience.[33] Each of these prospective normative aspects of experience (the linguistic, social, economic,
aesthetic, juridical, ethical, and pistical) possesses its unique
inner meaning (modal kernel) and is in principle entitled to
independent development when pursued as cultural activities by human beings. In plainer terms, a given human community — call it the state — is in principle entitled to pursue
juridical cultural activities without interference from an
ecclesiastical community — the church — whose proper busi-
ness is the faith aspect of human experience. Again, the church
should neither attempt to dictate style to an artistic community legitimately engaged in independent aesthetic cultural
activity, nor legislate "just prices" to an economic community,
equally entitled to independent development of its cultural
domain. The principle that appropriate human communities
should freely and independently pursue their corresponding

32. *New Critique*, pp. 184-188, 250-251, 265-268.
33. In relation to the normative functions above it in the "temporal
horizon of experience," Dooyeweerd would call the historical function
a "guided or directed meaning function" and the former the "guiding
or directing functions." See *New Critique*, pp. 184-185.

cultural activities is of course usually far from any existing state of affairs. But any instance of the principle's factual realization Dooyeweerd unabashedly calls "progress"; hence his first and most important norm of cultural development is that of cultural differentiation.[34]

The remaining normative content of the historical aspect as revealed by its anticipatory moments can be indicated with greater dispatch.[35] As pathfinders in the process of cultural differentiation, outstanding individuals (they remind one of Hegel's "world-historical individuals") will necessarily play a conspicuous role. Thus, "individualism" becomes another of Dooyeweerd's norms governing historical development. Yet Dooyeweerd admonishes these carriers of cultural change to purge themselves of revolutionary tendencies and maintain some continuity with tradition. Thus "continuity" becomes another of Dooyeweerd's "objective norms" of cultural development, for what precise reason I am not entirely certain, unless it be that his "temporal experiential horizon" of experience is as a whole continuous and "mutually coherent." In any case, both the economic and aesthetic anticipations in the historical aspect reveal norms of basically the same sort, those of cultural economy and harmony. As the various areas of cultural activity are progressively "opened up" or differentiated, they tend to jostle each other and dispute over primacy. But the economic and aesthetic anticipations in the historical aspect reveal to Dooyeweerd that if progress is to continue, the various areas of cultural activity will have to get on with each other, or function economically and harmoniously.[36]

34. For Dooyeweerd's treatment of the norm of diversification as such, see esp. *New Critique*, pp. 259-262.
35. I skip over the historical aspect's anticipation of the linguistic and social functions, because neither seems to add anything very decisive to the sum of Dooyeweerd's norms governing historical development. Suffice it to say that as the historical opening-up process begins, the community in which it takes place invariably develops the use of written symbols or language, because it feels a need to record the real historical changes that begin to occur. Similarly, a society in the process of opening up will cease to be isolated and will invariably develop cultural contacts with other societies, thus revealing the social anticipation of the historical aspect. For Dooyeweerd's treatment of these anticipations, see *New Critique*, pp. 284-286; *Twilight*, pp. 107-108.
36. *New Critique*, pp. 272-290.

Hence the two additional norms, which "forbid any excessive expansion of the formative power of a particular cultural sphere at the expense of the others."[37] When any of these cultural spheres gains the upper hand, the juridical anticipation in the historical aspect is in turn revealed, because the bloated sphere either "dashes itself to pieces against the power of the other differentiated spheres" or, if these latter have lost their power to resist, brings about "the collapse of an entire culture."[38]

Unfortunately, we have not yet reached the modal anticipation of the faith aspect and its specific role in historical development. To that we must turn later. But Dooyeweerd has so far accumulated enough norms (he sums them all up as the "norm of cultural differentiation, integration and individualization") to enable us to sketch a pretty precise outline of his version of secular hell, the most reactionary state of affairs, and a more rough outline of his secular utopia, a hypothetical most progressive state of affairs. On the worst of all possible worlds Dooyeweerd speaks clearly enough himself:

> Until the cultural historical aspect of a human society discloses the anticipatory moments of its meaning, it shows itself to be in a rigid and primitive condition. Primitive cultures are enclosed in small and undifferentiated organized communities, such as clans and tribes, which display a strong tendency towards isolation. As long as such primitive societies maintain their isolation in history, there can be no question of cultural development in the sense in which it is understood in historiography proper.
>
> They display a totalitarian character, since they include their members in all the spheres of their personal life, and the temporal existence of the individual is completely dependent on membership of the family or sib, respectively, and of the tribal community. There is no room as yet for a differentiation of culture in the

37. *Twilight*, p. 108.
38. *New Critique*, p. 290. Unfortunately, Dooyeweerd nowhere gives an example of "the collapse of an entire culture" because of the undue expansion of a single cultural sphere. It would be intriguing in the highest degree to know, for example, what over-mighty sphere was responsible for the decline and fall of Roman civilization.

particular spheres of formative power, those, namely, of science, fine arts, commerce and industry, of state and church, and so forth. Since such undifferentiated communities fulfill all the tasks for which, on a higher level of civilization, particular organizations are formed, there is only one single undifferentiated sphere. A rigid tradition, often deified by a pagan belief, and anxiously guarded by the leaders of the group, has the monopoly of formative power. The development process by which such cultural communities are formed shows only analogies of the biotic phases of birth, ripening, adolescence, age and decline. The duration of their existence is dependent on that of the small popular and tribal communities by which they are sustained. They may vanish from the scene without leaving any trace in the history of mankind.[39]

At the opposite pole, Dooyeweerd's hypothetical best of all possible worlds seems to consist of a world of benevolent and unwarlike states or juridical communities, each containing a number of overlapping communities independently but harmoniously pursuing various cultural activities or tasks. The "structural principles" or "inner nature" of these communities (the state, the church, an industrial community, etc.) are invariable and forever fixed by God's law, but as "structural norms" that may be violated by man they assume various forms in the course of time. Dooyeweerd seems to be working here with something like eternal and changeless Platonic ideas of these communities, to which their presently dim and changing approximations will only conform at the end of the historical process.[40]

But no matter. Few of us would in any case disagree that Dooyeweerd's best of all possible worlds would constitute a highly agreeable state of affairs. Its relevance for the writing of history unfortunately seems more problematical. Perhaps, first, a few concrete examples would make it clearer what Dooyeweerd's "objective criterion to distinguish truly progressive from reactionary tendencies in history" would amount to in practice, as well as indicate some of the diffi-

39. *Twilight*, pp. 99-100, which is in turn merely a translation of two paragraphs in Dooyeweerd, "Mouvements progressifs et régressifs dans l'histoire," *La Revue reformée*, XXXVI (1958/4), 8.
40. *Twilight*, p. 103.

culties its application would entail.[41] During the late Middle Ages, for example, the kings of western Europe gradually built up their "courts" and thereby extended the domain of royal justice as opposed to feudal justice. Now Dooyeweerd's criterion would oblige the historian to regard this development as progressive. The right to administer justice ceased to be an attribute of feudal land tenure; consequently, the juridical and economic cultural functions were diversified. Similarly, the efforts of the eighteenth-century Enlightenment to construct a purely "natural" as opposed to a "supernatural" ethic must be applauded as progressive, because the ethical and pistical functions were thereby diversified. Again, the laicization of the state and its consequent separation from the church wherever and whenever this has occurred — in America during the Revolution, in Italy in 1870, in France in 1905, and so on — ought also to be regarded as progressive, because it resulted in the separation of the juridical from the pistical cultural functions.

Dooyeweerd himself gives us an example of a "reactionary" movement, that of the European Restoration after the defeat of Napoleon, which, he says, "strove for the restoration of the medieval feudal regime. . . ."[42] Now, to the best of my knowledge, no one during the Restoration era "strove for the restoration of the medieval feudal regime" if the term "feudal" be understood in anything like its exact sense.[43] But be that as it may, let us briefly consider the example of one of the most "reactionary" of Restoration personalities, that of Hughes Félicité de Lamennais, the *enfant terrible* of the French right, whose nostalgia for medieval ecclesiastical authority was not even satiated by the passage of the infamous law against sacrilege in 1825. Undoubtedly, Lamennais wanted the restored Bourbon monarchy to wield its "secular sword" in behalf of the papacy's "spiritual sword" in a way that neither Urban VIII nor Innocent III had ever realized. Yet it was precisely because Lamennais eventually realized that the Bourbon monarchy would never play the role he had assigned

41. *Twilight,* p. 106.
42. *Twilight,* p. 97.
43. See Marc Bloch, *Feudal Society,* tr. L. A. Monyon (Chicago, 1966), II, 441-452, esp. p. 448.

it that he came to advocate the republic and the total separation of church and state, a political program Dooyeweerd would have to regard as "progressive." Any attempt to categorize the thought of Lamennais by the use of Dooyeweerd's criteria would have to conclude that it was neither clearly progressive nor clearly reactionary, but somehow both at the same time.[44]

Moreover, the same could be said about all the examples previously cited. If during the fourteenth and fifteenth centuries the so-called new monarchs of western Europe generally made some headway toward centralizing the administration of justice, the means of violence and the collection of revenue at the expense of their quasi-feudal "over-mighty subjects," it was only the better themselves to wage war with their neighboring monarchs and indulge in violence on scales hitherto unknown — hardly a "progressive" development by Dooyeweerd's standards or anyone else's. Similarly, the "natural morality" of the eighteenth-century philosophers, while duly free of theological or "pistical" considerations, was founded in turn on considerations of pain and pleasure and thus confounded with the sensory aspect of human experience — a trend that culminated in Jeremy Bentham's utilitarianism — with the result that no "progress" was achieved. And if the separation of church and state wherever and whenever it occurred must be regarded as a "progressive" turn of events, it must be confessed that it was intimately related to the rise of nationalism, which in effect made the nation-state into an object of worship. Thus the juridical and pistical functions were no sooner diversified than they were once again confounded — this time, indeed, to the advantage of the state, but without any real "progress" having been made.

Is it perhaps permissible to generalize from these few examples to all historical events indiscriminately? Take any event or development you will, cajole its component facts as you please; but the application of Dooyeweerd's criteria seems inevitably condemned to the conclusion that it was at once "progressive" and "reactionary," with the result that

44. See Alec R. Vidler, *Prophecy and Papacy: A Study of Lamennais, the Church and the Revolution* (New York, 1954).

every event vainly runs in place and achieves no "progress." And aware though I am of the fallacy of composition, it seems hardly possible in this case to say more about history as a whole than can be said of any of its component parts. Certainly, cultural functions are more diversified these days than they were in the Middle Ages, but the Middle Ages seem to have possessed a good deal more "integration" or "cultural economy and harmony" than we enjoy.[45] And if the inevitable conclusion to all the foregoing is that we have made no progress, one might legitimately entertain doubts concerning the value of deploying Dooyeweerd's vast and unwieldy paraphernalia in the first place. Its only discernible result would seem to be the Germanization of the vocabulary of historical literature, which has heretofore heroically resisted such tendencies.

VI

It might be objected that we have achieved some progress in at least one limited area, that of science and technology, or our understanding of and control over nature. If this be regarded as a value — and it is possible to do so only by carefully separating our knowledge of nature and ability to control it from the uses to which this knowledge and ability are put — we may readily grant the point. It seems clear that Sir Isaac Newton was a better scientist than, say, Alfred the Great, and that Albert Einstein's understanding of the universe was more refined than that of Newton. It was moreover the obviously cumulative nature of scientific knowledge that, more than any other factor, gave rise to the idea of human progress sometime during the seventeenth century. Quite modest when propounded by Fontenelle, the idea assumed the extravagant proportion of a dogma of inevitable human perfectibility at the close of the eighteenth century in the hands of Condorcet, whose enthusiasm was not even damp-

45. Perhaps a note of regret and nostalgia can be detected in Dooyeweerd's remarks concerning "la décomposition de la culture écclésiastique unifiée, telle qu'on la trouve dans la civilisation occidentale au Moyen Age. . . . " ("Mouvements progressifs et régressifs dans l'histoire," p. 12).

ened by the imminent specter of the guillotine.[46] It is not my purpose to trace the many and strange metamorphoses the idea of progress has subsequently undergone, but simply to note that it was conceived by the rise of science, born during the seventeenth century, and though it suffered cruelly under the shock of Lisbon earthquakes and Calas affairs, became one of the salient features of modern thought.

Karl Löwith is generally right in maintaining that the modern idea of inevitable secular progress owes only a portion of its content to Christianity, that it really consists of a combination or "synthesis" — to use a favorite Dooyeweerdian term of anathema — of the Christian expectation of the eschaton and the Platonic and Stoic view of history as eternally recurrent or cyclic.[47] For their part, the earliest Christians had an expectation of Christ's imminent return so intense that it is vain to look among them for a real interest in secular history as such, to say nothing of a notion of secular, cultural progress. It is true that with the gradual spread and acceptance of Christianity, and especially after the conversion of the emperor Constantine, certain Christian apologists, notably Eusebius, but also Jerome, Lactantius, and others, developed something like a Christian view of progress that saw the material stability and security of the *Pax Romana* as consequent on the success of Christianity. After the sack of Rome in 410, however, Saint Augustine vigorously opposed all such attempts to link Christianity with the success of any earthly state or civilization and radically separated the *civitas Dei* (city of God) from the historical vicissitudes of the *civitas terrena* (city of this world). If after the revelation of Christ any progress occurred in the former, it had solely to do with the salvation of sinners; as for the latter, far from being in any sense a medium for the progressive realization of the Kingdom of God, it presented nothing to the great saint ex-

46. See, in general, J. B. Bury, *The Idea of Progress: An Inquiry into Its Origin and Growth,* Dover edition (New York, 1955), esp. pp. 50-216; and on Turgot and Condorcet in particular, see Frank E. Manuel, *The Prophets of Paris,* Harper Torchbook edition (New York, 1962), pp. 13-102.
47. Karl Löwith, *Meaning in History,* Phoenix books edition (Chicago, 1957), esp. pp. 1-19, 161-203.

cept a linear sequence of the rise and fall of earthly powers and principalities ending abruptly and brutally in the second coming of Christ and the Last Judgment.

In so stating the case, Augustine was really groping his way back to the Hebrew and early Christian views on the matter, which came in turn to dominate the medieval atti- tude toward history and, at least in the various Augustinian confessional traditions, Christian thinking on the subject to the present day.[48] In view of this, Dooyeweerd's manifest belief in at least the possibility of cultural progress in terms of his conception of the Kingdom of God appears to be a deviation from the Augustinian tradition and a variety of "synthesis" — if I am permitted the term — between Chris- tianity and the modern notion of secular progress. As such it tends to link the cause of the Kingdom of God, however it be conceived, with those of particular historical states of affairs, a disadvantage of which Saint Augustine was painfully aware after the sack of Rome, and against which Calvinist Chris- tians ought especially to be on their guard after the not alto- gether edifying examples of the Cromwellian "revolution of the saints" and Puritan New England.[49] To my mind, it more- over deprives the Christian historian of one of his chief advan- tages: that is, since he lays up his treasure not on earth but in heaven, he can afford a great deal more honesty about the history of the former. Is it not far wiser and altogether more agreeable to Christianity, as Herbert Butterfield puts it, "to hold to Christ, and for the rest be totally uncommitted"?[50]

48. See *Meaning in History,* pp. 160-190; also Theodore E. Mommsen, "St. Augustine and the Christian Idea of Progress: The Background to the City of God," *Journal of the History of Ideas,* XII, 3 (June 1951), 346- 374, where some of Beard's more sweeping generalizations about the total absence of the idea of progress in classical, early Christian, and medieval thought are corrected.
49. Michael Walzer, *The Revolution of the Saints: A Study in the Origins of Radical Politics* (New York, 1968). On Calvinism as a radical revolu- tionary movement, see also H. G. Koenigsberger, "The Organization of Revolutionary Parties in France and The Netherlands during the Six- teenth Century," *Journal of Modern History,* XXVII (1955), 335-351.
50. Herbert Butterfield, *Christianity and History,* Fontana books (Lon- don, Glasgow, 1964), p. 189. Elsewhere in the same chapter, "History, Religion and the Present Day," Butterfield has some immensely sensible things to say that seem to me highly applicable to Dooyeweerd's philoso-

But aside from the question of the possibility of cultural progress — a belief to which Dooyeweerd manifestly adheres — a far more intriguing question arises: does Dooyeweerd believe that on the whole we are making progress or, to put it more bluntly, that progress in his terms is inevitable in the long run? Will history itself be the medium for the realization of the Kingdom of God? Dooyeweerd does not respond to this question explicitly, and his implicit responses are unfortunately ambivalent. In one breath he assures us optimistically that "there would be no future hope for mankind and for the whole process of man's cultural development if Jesus Christ had not become the spiritual center and his Kingdom the ultimate end of world-history," and that "this center will lead the new mankind as a whole to its true destination, since it has conquered the world by the divine love revealed in its self-sacrifice."[51] In another breath, however, he warns us that "the Christian can never agree with an optimistic view of cultural progress" because "the historical power of sin must also develop in an increasing degree," that the "historical opening-up process is marked by blood and tears," and that "it does not lead to an earthly paradise."[52]

Warnings against undue optimism and talk of Churchillean "blood, toil, sweat, and tears" might yet be conceivably reconciled with a belief in the ultimate inevitability of cultural progress. After all, who among the modern prophets of secular progress — including Turgot, Condorcet, Hegel, Marx, or Toynbee — has not cautioned us that its path would be strewn with mangled corpses, disemboweled women, burnt villages, and entire gutted civilizations, but that it would all be worth it in the end? But what is one then to make of the following black prognosis:

> In the factual course of history there is even no positive guarantee that the struggle for power is instrumental to a higher cultural justice in the sense that the culturally superior is destined to win.

phy of history, and on which I have heavily depended in my few remarks above.

51. *Twilight*, pp. 111-112.
52. *New Critique*, p. 262; *Twilight*, p. 111.

Such a view would ignore the working of sin in history. It may occur that what is culturally superior is conquered by what is inferior. In our sinful world the course of history is often marked by blood and tears, and in the struggle for power the principles of justice are often trampled down. But doubtless in the opening process the deepened historical *principles* become manifest which anticipate the meaning of retribution.[53]

Is this as much as to tell us that the historical process will not after all lead to the promised land, but that its value is chiefly to teach us lessons about the consequences of antinormative cultural behavior? If taken, of course, in a very general sense — that is, not in particular as an endorsement of Dooyeweerd's specific conception of normative cultural behavior — what Christian could disagree?

We seem to have gotten ourselves into a kind of Pascalian dilemma in which reason — at least Dooyeweerd's reason — pronounces both for and against the case of inevitable cultural progress, so that it is left to Dooyeweerd's "heart" to decide. In the last analysis, my guess (and it is only a guess) is that Dooyeweerd's "heart" decides against the case of inevitable cultural progress, that his historical process does not lead to the promised land. This last analysis entails a final weary ascent to cultural development's anticipation of the faith aspect of our experience, that "transcendental terminal sphere of the whole process of disclosure," and to its specific role in this process. Now although this faith aspect is a temporal cultural function like all the rest, Dooyeweerd describes it as "the opened window of time through which the light of God's eternity should shine into the whole temporal coherence of the world."[54] As such it is that cultural function which in the first instance is given its direction by the relationship between the central human self or "heart" and God, whether this relation be correct or apostate. The faith function in turn gives direction or guidance to the normative cultural functions

53. *New Critique,* p. 289.
54. *New Critique,* p. 302. For Dooyeweerd's general discussion of the faith aspect and its role in historical disclosure, see pp. 298-318.

below it in the "foundational direction of time," with the curious result that although these normative cultural functions — including the faith function — depend for their full disclosure on the opening-up of the historical aspect, the historical opening-up process depends for its direction or guidance on the normative cultural functions above it in the "transcendental direction of time," and ultimately, of course, on the faith aspect itself.[55]

This Gordian knot of "foundational" and "transcendental" interdependencies I gladly leave to professional philosophers to unravel if they can. What is important for our purposes, rather, is to note that since the faith aspect is itself given direction by the central heart's relationship to God, and since in Western history this relationship has assumed only four general shapes (the correct creation-fall-redemption type and the three apostate ones), we once again encounter Dooyeweerd's four "basic religious motives" and their primal causal efficacy in the historical process. Or perhaps there is also a fifth, because Dooyeweerd sometimes speaks of an "extreme transcendental limit reached in the apostasy of faith," characteristic of very primitive tribal communities, in which the faith function fastens itself to the pre-logical aspects of our experience and hence "deifies the unknown forces of nature regulating life and death, fertility and barrenness," and maintains the normative anticipatory spheres of all these aspects in an undisclosed and therefore ahistorical state.[56] No harm is thereby done to the pre-logical functions of temporal creation as such — at least insofar as their normative anticipatory spheres are not concerned — because these are realized automatically, without human intervention. But Dooyeweerd repeatedly stresses that the disclosure of their normative, post-logical anticipations depends solely on the historical realization of the normative law spheres by the free, culture-forming activity of human beings (in other words, on the historical opening-up process) and that the full-bodied, diversified, and yet integrated disclosure of these latter ultimately depends on

55. On this peculiar state of affairs, see *New Critique*, esp. pp. 186-192.
56. *New Critique*, pp. 363-364. See also n. 39 above.

the proper, biblical relation between man's central ego or "heart" and its Creator.[57]

What this finally boils down to is that for real progress to occur in any part of the world its culture-formers must be Christians, and not just any kind of Christians, but effectively in the "grip" of the "creation-fall-redemption motive," because any synthesis between the latter and apostate elements will produce at best only a distorted and partial variety of progress.[58] Now it is hardly an exaggeration to say that this happy state of affairs has never really materialized in the past and now seems at least as remote as the restoration of the Merovingian dynasty in France. Nothing seems less rigid, automatic, or dogmatically necessary, then, than Dooyeweerd's theory of progress, whereat we nonetheless marvel. For if the only legitimate conclusion to be drawn from all the foregoing is that like mankind, so has "the worlds whole frame [been] quite out of joynt, almost created lame," very lame and with no impending prospect of its taking up its bed and walking progressively, it seems an excessively mountainous philosophical labor to engender such a mouse-like result.[59] We come away feeling disappointed, even cheated. After so laboriously mounting the rungs of Dooyeweerd's "temporal horizon of experience," we had at least expected to be greeted by the music of the spheres if not a chorus of angels. But instead we find ourselves unceremoniously flung

57. "In the pre-logical aspects of reality the modal laws are realized in the facts without human intervention, at least insofar as in this realization the normative anticipations of their modal structure are not concerned. It is an essential characteristic of genuine modal norms that they do not realize themselves in this way. They only offer a rule of conduct to human judgement, a principle requiring human formation for its further specification" (*New Critique,* pp. 237-238). This view enables Dooyeweerd elsewhere to call the pre-normative or pre-logical spheres of experience "lois de la nature," as opposed to the normative spheres, which, again, require free human activity for their realization. See "Mouvements progressifs et régressifs dans l'histoire," p. 6.

58. On these various forms of distorted and partial progress characteristic, in Dooyeweerd's opinion, of Western history since the "opening-up" process began in ancient Mesopotamia, Greece, and Rome, see in general *New Critique,* pp. 319-365.

59. The quotation is from John Donne's "An Anatomy of the World," lines 191-192.

headlong into the slough of Henry Ford's history of "one damned thing after another."

If our guess is correct, if such is the ultimately pessimistic conclusion of Dooyeweerd's philosophy of history, then he merely reiterates the conviction of Christians of all ages that if only the world were truly Christian, if only it were uncontaminated by the effects of sin, the lion would lie down with the lamb, swords would be beat into plowshares and spears into pruning hooks. But alas! he must also in the end join them in bewailing the fact that, far from gradually approaching such a state of affairs, the lion will probably soon be extinct and hence unable to lie down with the lamb even were he so disposed, and the little remaining ore in the world will be surely used to make the modern equivalents of swords and spears from whose rusting hulks we can perhaps salvage a few plowshares and pruning hooks.

But who can say? Perhaps things will not be so, and perhaps what Dooyeweerd is really saying is that he believes that at some future date the world's cultural leaders will come under the sway of the creation-fall-redemption motive, under whose guidance they will bring the historical process safely into the port of the promised land. In this case, however, Dooyeweerd's idea of progress becomes an article of faith in a thing unseen (a turn of events yet to occur) and therefore a kind of eschatology. I will not pursue him into the sanctuary of eschatology if he wishes to take refuge there, except to observe that if his idea of progress has only an eschatological content, it is of dubious usefulness to the historian, who by definition concerns himself with the past.[60]

It might yet be objected that the simple criteria of lions lying down with lambs and the like are naive and "prescientific," and that what Dooyeweerd has accomplished is at least to provide us with a set of precisely defined, objective criteria with which to distinguish a truly and unambiguously

60. Of course, Dooyeweerd does not agree that the historian is "by definition" concerned with the past. By Dooyeweerd's definition the historian is concerned with the "historical aspect" of things and events, presumably whether they be past, present, or future. It would therefore seem to follow from this definition that the historian could indeed concern himself with at least an aspect of eschatology.

progressive historical development should one ever occur. But these criteria or norms also prove to be problematical when examined by themselves; and here we undoubtedly reach the crux of the matter. Recall that "diversification" is one of his chief norms by which to distinguish progressive from reactionary events. Now why this curious attribution of superiority to temporal diversity as opposed to temporal unity? Dooyeweerd claims to derive this norm from the so-called cultural mandate in Genesis, but try as I may, I cannot find it there, either explicitly or implicitly. The biblical injunction to have dominion over the earth, though it might entitle one to consider scientific and technological achievement progressive as such, carries with it absolutely no stipulation as to the organization of this cultural effort, whether to be undertaken by a single community or diverse communities.[61] At this point the Tower of Babel incident seems to come to Dooyeweerd's rescue. To him it demonstrates that "seclusion and isolation in cultural development is contrary to the Divine ordinance" and that "cultural expansion, the spread of humanity over the surface of the earth in the differentiation of the cultural groups, and the cultural contact between these groups, have been set as a task for mankind." Now this interpretation might hold some water if the community building the Tower of Babel had been only one among many, and had attempted to isolate itself from the others. But Scripture clearly intends this group to be representative of humanity as a whole: "The Lord said, Behold, the people is one, and they have all one language. . . ." Moreover, the Lord's response to this state of affairs was to "go down, and there confound their language, that they may not understand one another's speech," all of which surely renders Dooyeweerd's postulated mandate of "cultural contact between . . . groups" considerably more difficult. Finally, the Lord's avowed purpose in confounding their language was to prevent them from doing everything "which they have imagined to do," which would seem to indicate that he took a dim view of the cultural progress that cooperatively they might have achieved. Taken all in all, the purpose of the Tower of Babel

61. Gen. 1:28; *Twilight*, p. 91.

incident is vastly different from Dooyeweerd's interpretation, which at best represents highly dubious biblical exegesis.[62]

What seems to be guiding Dooyeweerd's thought here is not Scripture but the Platonic and neo-Platonic notion that the eternal one and changeless God is obliged by virtue of his very self-sufficiency to produce the greatest possible diversity of temporal effects, the notion Professor Lovejoy in *The Great Chain of Being* calls the "principle of plenitude." This principle is quite foreign to anything in biblical Christianity, although it was, to be sure, "synthesized" with Christian thinking at an early date. And as long as we are on this track, it is perhaps not wholly fanciful to see in Dooyeweerd's norm of "continuity" what Lovejoy calls the "principle of continuity," whose origin he locates in Aristotle's insistence that nature contained no sharp breaks or cleavages. If there is anything to all this — and I am strongly inclined to think there is — then Dooyeweerd again stands convicted of "synthesis."[63]

VII

For all Dooyeweerd's talk about history as a "science" with a delimited aspect of reality to investigate and "objective norms" of its own, his total view of the subject is nonetheless a comprehensive, intensely personal vision embracing the origin, development, present state, and destiny of mankind. As it happens, I do not entirely share this vision. To be sure, I partake in Dooyeweerd's faith in the final victory of Christ over the powers of darkness and in the coming of his kingdom. But I cannot, it seems, completely adhere to either his specific vision of that kingdom or his faith (if it is indeed a part of his faith, for the question remains very open in my

62. Gen. 11:1-9; *New Critique,* p. 262.
63. Arthur O. Lovejoy, *The Great Chain of Being: A Study of the History of an Idea,* Harper Torchbook edition (New York, 1960), pp. 24-66. For evidence of Dooyeweerd's indebtedness to late nineteenth- and early twentieth-century phenomenology, and in particular to the "post-neo-Kantians" Nicolai Hartman and James Feiblemann, see Dirk Jellema, "The Philosophy of Vollenhoven and Dooyeweerd," *The Calvin Forum,* April 1954, pp. 169-172; May 1954, pp. 192-194; October 1954, pp. 31-33.

mind) that the historical process will itself be the vehicle of its progressive realization. All the same, and in spite of the built-in indisposition of most historians in the face of architectonic philosophical systems, I would be insensitive indeed were I not possessed of at least a sneaking admiration for Dooyeweerd's philosophical articulation of this vision. Its simultaneously vast and detailed quality is as breathtaking in its way as a Gothic cathedral.

I would not willingly dismantle this cathedral. In any case, it is neither my purpose nor in my power to do so. What I have attempted to show is that what Herbert Butterfield calls "technical" or "academic" history — the painstaking enterprise of reconstructing segments of the past on the basis of the critical and exhaustive examination of manuscripts or other kinds of evidence — cannot legitimately be employed as its flying buttress.[64] Technical history simply cannot and will not support it and must necessarily crumble beneath its weight. The scientific study of the *civitas terrena* can be enlisted under the banner of Dooyeweerd's vision of the Kingdom of God only by outflanking vast quantities of some kinds of evidence here, roughly trampling down other kinds there — in short by either consciously or unconsciously indulging in a kind of intellectual dishonesty that no vision, however glorious, can really justify. If academic history be pressed into the service of Dooyeweerd's world-historical vision, then Christian historians can formulate no principial objection to its being pressed into other, quite alien world-historical causes, such as the Marxist one. I doubt very much that Dooyeweerdian history would fare very well in the ensuing competition. The "history of all hitherto existing society" as "the history of class struggles" leading to the classless society is bound to look better documented, more "scientific," and hence more persuasive than the equally dogmatic and exclusive history of all hitherto existing society as the history of struggles among "basic religious motives" leading to the diversified and integrated society. It seems to me altogether more prudent for the Christian historian to play the gadfly in

64. Herbert Butterfield, *Christianity and History*, p. 35, and in general pp. 19-35.

the historical profession, to abase academic history every time it is unduly exalted by reminding it unceasingly of what it cannot prove — or disprove — and of its severe limitations both in the kinds of evidence at its disposal and its all too blunt tools of analysis.

If thus released from service to Dooyeweerd's vision, is academic history to be regarded as completely "neutral," as an exercise in "autonomous theoretical thought"? This conclusion does not follow and is in any case untrue, although we do well to remind ourselves that historians of the most diverse persuasions can and do reach consensus on certain matters. Does it divorce the historian's faith from his profession as historian to make him into a "dualist" and an unwitting victim of the grace-nature basic religious motive? If merely to hold that the humble "craft of the historian" is by itself inadequate to the task of demonstrating the truth of Dooyeweerd's vision is necessarily to subscribe to a philosophical dualism, then so be it. But I doubt that this claim would bear serious philosophical scrutiny. Worse yet, does the rejection of Dooyeweerd's history make history into a meaningless "collection of diverse facts from the past"?[65] The accusation is Dooyeweerd's, and in the face of it my Pascalian instinct is now to exalt academic history when so unduly abased. Is there really no middle ground of meaning and significance between Dooyeweerd's history of the progressive realization of the Kingdom of God and Henry Ford's history of "one damned thing after another"? Surely there is, and the challenge of Dooyeweerd should spur us to find it.

65. "Collection de faits divers du passé." See "Mouvements progressifs et régressifs dans l'histoire," p. 2.

Christianity and History:
a Bibliographical Essay

M. HOWARD RIENSTRA

A BIBLIOGRAPHER'S first disclaimer is usually that his work is not exhaustive. Unfortunately, this present effort is so obviously not exhaustive that it would be pretentious to disclaim it. It pretends to be little more than a product of my personal interests and reading and of the shape of my personal Christian commitment. It is an introductory essay to a vast and constantly expanding literature on the varied and complex relationships between Christianity and history. In distinction from the more elaborate and competent bibliographies that have been published, the modest merit of this effort is to introduce the major questions that lie behind this vast literature, and to suggest starting points for reading on those major questions.

A bibliographer, however, must also establish with some clarity what he is about. What principles of inclusion and exclusion has he attempted to follow? There are two principles that control this essentially personal selection. The first principle is to limit entries to books and articles published after 1945. Although the topic is as old as the Bible, Eusebius, and St. Augustine, there is a qualitative as well as a quantitative change in the literature of the postwar years. The war had led to an open questioning of the continuing relevance of Christianity to civilization as well as to any form of scholarly endeavor. The response of Christian theologians such as Bultmann and Löwith and historians such as Butterfield and Latourette, was an explicit affirmation of such relevance and a deepening understanding of the concept of history and the historical. The second principle of selection arises directly out of this explicit quality of postwar literature. Only those writings that self-consciously reflect on the many relationships between Christianity and history are included in this essay. If not in the title, at least in the body of the piece, the concept of history or the historical must be present to be included, and even then only when in conjunction with Christianity. Many historians, philosophers, and theologians are Christians, and many of them have integrated their commitment to Christ with their scholarly activities. But the literature to be included in this essay is that which reflects on and discusses the relationship of Christ to historical, philosophical, and theological studies. For example, Lewis W. Spitz is an outstanding Christian historian who has not, to the best of my knowledge, written reflectively on the relationship of Christianity and history. Therefore, his name does not appear, even though in the doing of history he has contributed more than some whose names do appear.

History is a deceptively simple term with many meanings. There is history as it appears to all men and history as it appears to historians, philosophers, and theologians. History is something lived, and history is something written. History is the total past as it relates to man, and history is an account of that past. History is reality, and history is a science. History is an attempt to discover meaning and coherence in all human events as they are lived and experienced, but history is also the attempt by a present generation of scholars to discover meaning and coherence in human events both retrospectively and prospectively. There is, as these alternative meanings convey, a history for everyman and a history for scholars. The latter is an interpretation of the former. And each scholarly discipline has a sense of the meaning of history that is peculiar to the questions raised in that discipline. Each also has a distinct understanding of the relationship of Christianity to history. Therefore, I have divided this bibliography into three parts corresponding to the three disciplines primarily concerned with the topic Christianity and history, and each of the sections is introduced by a set of questions that define the concerns respectively of historians, philosophers, and theologians.

Before coming to that, however, I should acknowledge the availability of previous bibliographies on this topic. Many of the books and articles to be cited below contain bibliographies, and, in fact, several are actually extended bibliographical essays. In 1954 the first separately compiled bibliography on this topic was published by Charles P. Loughran, "Theology and History: A Bibliography," *Thought*, XXIX, (1954), 101-115. The periodical *Fides et Historia*, published by the Conference on Faith and History, publishes many articles and reviews related to this topic. An earlier version of this bibliography was published there under the title "The Problem of a Christian Philosophy of History," II, 1 (1969), 24-41. Most important of all is the periodical *History and Theory: Studies in the Philosophy of History*. Since 1960 it has published several very useful and complete bibliographies in addition to articles and reviews of the highest merit. The most recent of their bibliographies is specific to our topic: Robert North, S. J., compiler, "Bibliography of Works in Theology and History," *History and Theory*, XII, 1 (1973), 55-140. It lists works published since 1900, but the emphasis is on the period from 1945 to 1972. Since it is subdivided into four sections, its usefulness is enhanced by an author index at the end. *History and Theory* has made an editorial commitment to a series of bibliographies under the general title "Bibliography of Works in the Philosophy of History." The following have been published: John C. Rule, "1945-1957" (Supplement 1, 1961); M. Nowicki, "1958-1961" (Supplement 3, 1964); Lewis Wurgaft et al., "1962-1965" (Supplement 7, 1967) and "1966-1968" (Supplement 10, 1970); Astrid Witschi-Bernz, "1500-1800" (Supplement 12, 1972).

A. *Christianity and History for Historians*

The crisis within the boundaries of a nominally Christian civilization that was occasioned by the Communist and fascist revolutions, the holocaust, and the Second World War, led to a critical questioning of the relevance of Christian faith to life and learning. Was the Christian faith as the spiritual dynamic of Western civilization now dead? What was the role of the Christian and of the Christian church? Was the Christian faith to be relegated to a category of obsolescence? Could history be construed or interpreted any longer in a

Christian way? Were not Christian interpretations now merely childish myths or fairy tales as they were compared to the harsher and more mature secular ideologies? Was a Christian historian anything more than a craftsman-scholar who curiously held to a personal faith despite all the evidence of its irrelevance? By 1948 and 1949 the responses and the reaffirmations of a Christian position were beginning to be heard. Historians first articulated these responses in America and England.

The 1948 presidential address to the American Historical Association was given by an evangelical, Kenneth Scott Latourette, under the title "The Christian Understanding of History," *American Historical Review*, LIV (1949), 259-267. Latourette said that his faith was integral to his work as an historian. He saw no reason to hide his presuppositions. The Christian vision of history is even compatible, as Latourette saw it, with some constructions of the idea of progress. But equally important was that he as president of the American Historical Association said that Christian faith and academic history could be integrated. E. Harris Harbison (see below) was later to acknowledge the loneliness of the Christian historian among his professional colleagues until Latourette and others began articulating a positive position for the Christian faith.

In England, Hugh F. Kearney wrote "Christianity and the Study of History," *Downside Review*, LXVII (1949), 62-75. But the magisterial effort was the 1948 lectures of Herbert Butterfield, given to Cambridge students, subsequently published as *Christianity and History* (London: Bell, 1949), and reprinted many times since. Butterfield affirmed the relevance of Christian faith even to the minute details of historical scholarship, and cautioned against a too facile identification of the historian's personal moral judgments with God's judgments in history. Butterfield sensed a spiritual dynamic at work in the entire secular process. This led him to affirm that a religious — not an ecclesiastical — interpretation of history seems both acceptable and correct.

Christopher Dawson, a Catholic historian-sociologist, had asserted the centrality of a religious dynamic to history as early as 1929 and again in 1938. His pre- and postwar essays on this theme are collected in *The Dynamics of World History* (London: Sheed & Ward, 1956). Dawson was sensitive to the Christian's role as intellectual. He understood both the academic and the political consequences of what he called the new ideologies of history, particularly the Marxist. He wished to counter this vogue of ideological interpretation by affirming the continuing validity of the Christian view. Dawson's Gifford lectures of 1948-49 are his most effective demonstration of the Christian interpretive thesis: *Religion and the Rise of Western Culture* (London: Sheed & Ward, 1950).

Dawson was aware that a more critical test of a Christian interpretation of history would be to apply it to Eastern or Oriental civilization. René Grousset, a French Catholic orientalist, attempted just that. In bitter, almost cynical, postwar despair, Grousset published *Bilan de l'Histoire* (Paris: Blon, 1946). It was translated by A. and H. Temple Patterson under the title, *The Sum of History* (London: Tower Bridge, 1951). It is simultaneously a plea for Christian witness to the world and for a Christian interpretation of world history. In despair Grousset calls Christians to proclaim salvation in Christ. The role of Christians in world history is to proclaim the salvation available outside world history. A similar effort to understand the role of Christians and Christianity in both Eastern and Western civilization has been undertaken more recently by the Protestant anthropologist-historian Arend Th. van Leeuwen, *Christianity in World History* (New York: Scribners, 1965; Dutch original, 1964). In his brilliant development of many questions and insights van Leeuwen too is pleading for a Christian understanding of world history. What is the Christian's role now that Western civilization has become secularized? Can the witness of the Christian be separated from this now secularized identity? Whereas Grousset anticipates the consequences of Christian mission to lie outside or beyond history, van Leeuwen anticipates consequences within history. Both books present fascinating challenges to Christian historians.

To continue the theme of the Christian role in history, we may perhaps be permitted to mention one theologian

among these many historians. In 1945, John Baillie presented
the Riddell lectures on the topic *What is Christian Civilization?* (London, 1945). Sensitive to the current theological
themes of crisis, tragedy, and paradox, Baillie struggles to
discover a Christian presence in Western civilization. He concludes with the admonition that all civilization falls under
God's judgment. Also on the theme of Christianity and its
unique role in Western civilization is a slim book by Carlton
J. H. Hayes, *Christianity and Western Civilization* (Stanford:
University Press, 1954). His portrayal of a religious dynamic,
following the tradition of Dawson, is marred only by a too
easy identification of that dynamic with purely humanitarian
traditions.

A collection of the essays of E. Harris Harbison, *Christianity and History* (Princeton: University Press, 1964) is
valuable on several counts. He approaches an Augustinian
view of the relationship of God to history, and he chronicles
the postwar developments in both history and theology—both
Protestant and Catholic — that gave Christian historians new
confidence. Among others, there is a useful essay on Calvin's
sense of history. Unfortunately, Harbison resorts to too vague
a sense of Christianity when he mistakenly identifies Arnold
Toynbee as a practicing Christian. Page Smith, *The Historian
and History* (New York: Knopf, 1964), clearly summarizes
the role of recent philosophy and theology in the definition
of the historian's task, but his personal conclusion about the
usefulness of a "sense of history as the unfolding of time
pregnant with Divine potentiality" (p. 248) is unworthy of
Eugene Rosenstock-Huessy, to whom his book is dedicated.
Still worthy of study is the short essay by Paul Ward, who
was later to become the Executive Director of the American
Historical Association, entitled "The Christian and History
Teaching," *Religion in Life*, XXVI (1957), 490-500.

Helpful as a caution to historians who might oversimplify
the relationship of Christianity to history is M. C. Smit's in-
augural lecture at the Free University of Amsterdam, *The
Divine Mystery in History* (Kampen: Kok, 1955). Similarly
concerned with mystery is the compact essay on the implications of recent developments in philosophy and theology for

the historian's work by Georges Florovsky, "The Predicament of the Christian Historian," in *Religion and Culture: Essays in Honor of Paul Tillich*, ed. W. Leibrecht (New York: Harper, 1959). While affirming Christ to be truly the Lord of history, Florovsky concludes that the Christian historian will find history to be "a mystery and tragedy — a mystery of salvation and a tragedy of sin" (p. 166).

To conclude this section on history for historians, I should note several essays that appeared during the sixties. Henri I. Marrou, "From the Logic of History to an Ethic for the Historian," *Cross Currents*, Winter, 1961, 61-77, is by an historian of St. Augustine and ancient education. The venerable James T. Shotwell has a chapter entitled "Christianity and History" in his *The Faith of an Historian* (New York: Walker, 1964), pp. 94-122. There is the delightful essay by Albert C. Outler, "Theodosius's Horse: Reflections on the Predicament of the Church Historian," *Church History*, XXXIV (1965), 251-261. Jeffrey Russell, "Religious Commitment and Historical Writing," *The Christian Scholar*, XLV (1962), 11-21, is a concise statement of a specific problem; C. Gregg Singer, "The Nature of History," in *Christian Faith and Modern Theology*, ed. Carl F. H. Henry (New York: Channel Press, 1964), is discursive and theological even though written by an historian.

B. *Christianity and History for Philosophers*

There are two kinds of questions appropriate to this section. There are questions that arise out of what is called critical, sometimes analytical, philosophy of history, and questions that arise out of speculative philosophy of history. Critical philosophy of history presents the following questions: What is the nature of historical knowledge? Is history a unique form of inquiry with a unique kind of explanation? Is historical explanation scientific or narrative? How do the historian's personal situation and intellectual commitments influence his explanation? Is objectivity possible? Can historical generalizations and interpretations be verified? Speculative philosophy of history, on the other hand, presents the following questions: Does history have meaning? Are there patterns in history that can be discerned? Is there an origin and goal to history? Are there general theories that are adequate to render the confusing multiplicity of historical events intelligible or meaningful? Is the ground for such theories intrinsic to history? Or is the only adequate ground perhaps extrinsic and essentially religious? If so, are all philosophies of history then actually theologies of history?

Questions of critical and speculative philosophy of history merge at one critical point. Is historical knowledge adequate ground for a speculative philosophy, or even theology, of history? Some Christian philosophers and historians have been led to consider questions arising in the area of critical philosophy of history because of this problem. Usually, however, these questions are raised only in the course of commenting on secular philosophies of history, or in the formulation of a Christian alternative. An example of this is the work of John Warwick Montgomery, *The Shape of the Past* (Ann Arbor: Edwards, 1962), a forceful critique of secular philosophies of history and an affirmation of the adequacy of historical methodology for Christian apologetic. Montgomery's work led Ronald Nash, in "The Use and Abuse of History in Christian Apologetic," *Christian Scholar's Review*, I, 3 (1971), 217-226, to examine some questions about the nature of historical knowledge; responses appear in I, 4 (1971), 325-331 and 332-335. The nature of historical inquiry is also addressed in response to Montgomery by Ronald J. Vander Molen, *Fides et Historia*, III, 1 (1970), 41-51, followed by an exchange, IV, 2 (1972), 85-93 and V, 1 (1973), 109-112. Earl William Kennedy renews the discussion in *Fides et Historia*, V, 1-2 (1973), 117-121, which brought another response and rejoinder in VII, 1 (1974), 26-36.

The relationship of Christianity to history for philosophers is more typically expressed in the questions arising out of speculative philosophy of history. The two seminal works of the postwar period that dramatically influenced the understanding of Christianity's relationship to speculative philosophy of history were both written by theologians: Karl Löwith and Reinhold Niebuhr. Löwith's *Meaning in History: The*

Theological Implications of the Philosophy of History (Chicago: University Press, 1949) argues that all modern speculative philosophies of history are nothing more than secularized versions of the biblical view of history and of Christian eschatology. By tracing this process of secularization backward from Marx and Hegel to St. Augustine and the Bible, Löwith demonstrates how eschatological hope has been transformed into a secular vision of progress and of earthly utopias. Niebuhr's *Faith and History: A Comparison of Christian and Modern Views of History* (New York: Scribners, 1949) mounts a similar attack. Modern philosophies of history are oversimplifications of reality because they have taken the Christian ideas of love, hope, and freedom and tried to absolutize them into history while forgetting sin. Marxism, for example, is "a secularized version of sectarian perfectionism" (p. 209). Niebuhr takes history seriously, but he is critical of all philosophies of history precisely because they are impositions on historical reality of the rational categories of the modern mind. The Christian view is more consistent with history as lived and recorded because it takes into account tragedy and paradox.

Martin C. D'Arcy, S. J., *The Meaning and Matter of History: A Christian View* (New York: Farrar, 1959), also emphasizes paradox, but from a Catholic point of view. In his survey of the rise of modern philosophy of history, he is less severe in his judgments than Löwith and Niebuhr. Accepting their temporal and temporary reasonableness, he rather notes that all are insufficient from the Christian viewpoint. The bulk of this book, however, is a statement on a topic of the theology of history, and will be mentioned in that section. A Christian interpretation of the history of the philosophy of history — both speculative and critical — is given in John Edward Sullivan, *Prophets of the West: An Introduction to the Philosophy of History* (New York: Holt, 1970). Sullivan also notes the secularizing process in its development, but then notes the general abandonment of speculative philosophies of history under the impact of criticism from historians and philosophers alike. He ends his account with a presentation of Teilhard de Chardin's Christian evolutionism. He holds it to be a philosophy of history based on a simple Christian faith as illumined by the intellectual visions of the mid-twentieth century. There is meaning in the vision of Teilhard, but is not this philosophy of history now in fact a theology of history?

One very curious effort to discern meaning in history without basing it on a theology of history is by Alban G. Widgery, *The Meanings in History* (London: Allen, 1967). Widgery seems to be an old-style liberal who still believes that reason unaided can yet discover ultimate truth. He argues that all dimensions of personal experience, when properly assessed, lead to the conclusion that life — and therefore history — is meaningful. Even the existence of God is a reasonable inference from human experience. It is reasonable to posit the existence of God, as it turns out, because he has been such an essential part of the history of world religions (p. 108). Although hardly satisfying to the Christian, the book should be noted as a late attempt to find meaning in history apart from ideological commitment and without invoking either faith or revelation. The issue of faith and revelation in relation to a philosophy of history is rather perversely addressed in a book by G. L. Keyes, *Christian Faith and the Interpretation of History: A Study of St. Augustine's Philosophy of History* (Lincoln: University of Nebraska, 1966). Keyes repeatedly attacks St. Augustine for "beginning with certain *a priori* premises which he attributes to divine revelation" (p. 85). Since all religious beliefs come from sensations, and since religious beliefs are central to his interpretation of history, St. Augustine's philosophy of history is a product of his confusion of a subjective feeling of certainty with truly verifiable knowledge. Keyes concludes that St. Augustine's philosophy of history "is fatal to historical studies as pursued by men of open mind" (p. 194).

Since most of those cited in this section have been theologians, we may note with satisfaction that at least one Christian philosopher has addressed himself to the problems of the philosophy of history, both speculative and critical: Gordon H. Clark, *Historiography: Secular and Religious* (Nutley, N. J.: Craig, 1971). Clark treats both secular and religious theories of history; by the former he means primarily theories on the nature of historical knowledge. He generally accepts the demise of scientific historiography and cheers the abandonment of objectivity. He does, however, insist on the necessity of moral judgments. Unfortunately, Clark fails to establish a unified or coherent approach of his own. The book is more an extended bibliographical essay with strange excursions into technical analysis than it is a systematic monograph. In distinction from Clark's, the philosophy of Herman Dooyeweerd is coherent and systematic, even though underdeveloped on history. Two critical articles have recently appeared that may open discussion to a more positive end: Nick Van Til, "Dooyeweerd's 'History' and the Historian," *Pro Rege* [Dordt College], II, 1 (1973); Earl William Kennedy, "Herman Dooyeweerd on History: An Attempt to Understand Him," *Fides et Historia*, VI, 1 (1973), 1-21. The reader will be rewarded to discover in that same issue of *Fides et Historia* two articles on Arnold Toynbee: William W. Paul, "Toynbee's View of Christianity" (22-29), and Sherman B. Barnes, "The Personal Religion of Arnold J. Toynbee" (30-35). These two articles elicited a generally concurring response from Toynbee, which was published as "Toynbee on Toynbee," *Fides et Historia*, VI, 2 (1974), 66-67.

C. *Christianity and History for Theologians*

The problem of understanding the relationship of Christianity to history in this context arises out of the deceptively simple proposition that Christianity is an historical religion. This seems to refer to the fact that man's response to God is worked out in the temporal-historical order, and that God himself in Christ both entered and redeemed the whole creation. Thus history is significant. But a bewildering array of questions follows. If Christianity is historical, are the truth claims of Christianity subject to verification through historical inquiry? Or does the truth of Christianity rest solely on faith? Are there two types of history, *Historie* and *Geschichte*, with *Historie* being the events and facts of the past and *Geschichte* their interpretation? If so, is *Historie* the past as subject to historical inquiry and *Geschichte* the salvational meaning of those events as apprehended by faith? Does this entail a sharp distinction between profane or secular history and sacred or salvation history (*Heilsgeschichte*)? Is there then also a Jesus of history that is distinct from the kerygmatic Christ, the Christ of faith? And how important is the temporal and historical, over against the eternal and eschatological? What is the significance of historical existence? Is the meaning of history "inside" — transformational and incarnational views — or "outside" — ascetic and eschatological views?

To explore the full meaning of these questions in twentieth-century philosophy and theology would require much more than a bibliographical essay. There are three books that may serve to introduce the reader to the background of these questions. E. C. Rust, *Towards a Theological Understanding of History* (New York: Oxford, 1963) is the most conventional explanation both in terms of its vocabulary and theology. James M. Connolly, *Human History and the Word of God* (New York: Macmillan, 1965), presents a detailed account of the philosophical origins from a Catholic perspective. The special merit of this book, however, is that it contains two brilliant chapters on Protestant and Catholic theologies of history. Connolly clarifies those distinct traditions in both Protestant and Catholic thought that lead to the options that affirm or deny the significance of the historical. The same options are clarified in slightly different terms in the classical work of H. Richard Niebuhr, *Christ and Culture* (New York: Harper, 1951). In the tradition of H. Richard Niebuhr and Karl Rahner is Van Harvey's affirmation of what he calls a "radical historical confessionalism." Although not specifically a survey like the previously cited three, Harvey's *The Historian and the Believer: The Morality of Historical Knowledge* (New York: Macmillan, 1966) is particularly useful for an analysis of what he calls "hard and soft perspectivism." This is a discussion of Ernst Troeltsch and historical relativism and how it influences the major questions about history for theologians.

An ecumenical approach to the problems of the theology of history in the postwar period was opened in 1949 at Chateau de Bossey. The papers are published in a volume entitled *On the Meaning of History* (Geneva: Oikumene, 1949). Prof. Th. Preiss, "The Vision of History in the New Testatment," argues for the significance of the time between the Incarnation and the Judgment in which the Christian is called to social responsibility. Jean Danielou, S. J., "The Conception of History in the Christian Tradition," finds this same history to be at best ambiguous. The tension between "in but not of" and "even now — not yet" is more fully elaborated in Danielou's book *The Lord of History* (Chicago: Regnery, 1958), where he finds even the historical church to be a subject sphere of the demonic. Danielou thus identifies himself with an eschatological interpretation of history. That position is decisively not shared by Reinhold Niebuhr or Father Martin D'Arcy in their books cited above. Niebuhr certainly expects judgment, and he recognizes the distorting effects of sin, but he insists on the significance of the Christian's struggle in history despite its paradoxical and sometimes tragic outcome. D'Arcy is even more emphatically a representative of the incarnationalist position in Catholic theology. While doubting the possibility of a Christian philosophy of history, he distinctly affirms a theology of history with Christ as the focal point. For a very succinct statement of the theology of the Catholic incarnationalist point of view, one should consult Karl J. Rahner, "Christianity and the New Earth," in *Knowledge and the Future of Man*, ed. Walter J. Ong, S. J. (New York: Holt, 1968).

Karl Löwith, however, is a Protestant who accepts Karl Barth's distinction between *Historie* and *Geschichte* and thus denies any meaning or value to human history. Jesus Christ is God's grace in history, but the full reconciliation of man to God lies outside history and is known only through faith. For an explanation of the critically different positions of Ernst Troeltsch and Karl Barth on history, one should consult Thomas W. Ogletree, *Christian Faith and History* (New York: Abingdon, 1965). The one work of Protestant theology that has had the greatest impact on the understanding of the Christian view of history is Rudolf Bultmann, *History and Eschatology: The Presence of Eternity* (New York: Harper,

1957). Influenced by Collingwood and others, Bultmann adopted a radical historical relativist position and fitted it into his existentialism. This led him to affirm the present meaningfulness of eschatological hope in the paradox of Christian existence: human history as history has no meaning. His student Friedrich Gogarten, in *Demythologizing and History* (London: SCM, 1955), and later in an article, "The Unity of History," *Theology Today*, XV, 2 (1958), rejects the distinction between *Historie* and *Geschichte*, between sacred and profane, and locates a now demythologized faith totally within history. An even stronger rejection of the distinction between *Historie* and *Geschichte* in favor of a "loving union" between the sacred and the profane is found in W. Taylor Stevenson, *History as Myth: The Import for Contemporary Theology* (New York: Seabury, 1969). But here history is myth and faith is encounter. Also useful in this context is a collection of essays edited by Carl E. Braaten, *New Directions in Theology Today, Vol. 2: History and Hermeneutics* (Philadelphia: Westminster, 1966). And for a vigorous critique of the traditions of both Barth and Bultmann, John Warwick Montgomery's previously cited book and many articles are always interesting.

Oscar Cullmann is a biblical theologian who sees Jesus Christ as the midpoint in history. In his early work *Christ and Time* (Philadelphia: Westminster, 1950), he explicated the linear view of time to which Christ is central. In his more recent *Salvation in History* (London: SCM, 1967), he contends that all history is to be understood in the light of salvation history. The Christian's knowledge of the "not yet," when combined with his knowledge of the "already," leads to a consciousness of "being fellow-workers in carrying out the saving plan in history" (p. 338). Thus history has meaning through the understanding of God's saving purposes in Christ and through human responsibility to realize those purposes in time. Hendrikus Berkhof, *Christ the Meaning of History* (Richmond: John Knox, 1966) is in a similar theological tradition. Berkhof finds the cross and resurrection of Christ as the key to understanding the present and the future.

The centrality of Christ as seen from a Catholic perspective is concisely expressed by Hans Urs von Balthasar, *A Theology of History* (London: Sheed & Ward, 1963). A more comprehensive Catholic evaluation of both Protestant and Catholic theologies of history is found in Osmund Lewry, O.P., *The Theology of History* (Notre Dame: Fides, 1969). For a more elementary view and a Protestant perspective, one might consult Howard Grimes, *The Christian Views History* (New York: Abingdon, 1969). While slight on theology, the merit of Grimes' book is that he considers related questions, such as the role of the church and the teaching of history. Finally, there are two Protestant theologians who stand very close to the traditions of Cullmann and Berkhof. Roger L. Shinn, *Christianity and the Problem of History* (New York: Scribners, 1953), finds history to be a progression of faith in the Augustinian sense. Alan Richardson, *History Sacred and Profane* (London: SCM, 1964), returns to the theme of a Christian apologetic in relation to the sufficiency of historical evidence for the Incarnation and resurrection. His effort is to reconcile the Jesus of history to the Christ of faith.

There is a vast and specialized literature on this latter problem. One could well begin with James M. Robinson, *A New Quest of the Historical Jesus* (London: SCM, 1959). For a fuller explanation of the older quests for the historical Jesus, one should consult Charles C. Anderson, *Critical Quests of Jesus* (Grand Rapids: Eerdmans, 1969). A collection of articles on the problem has been edited by Carl E. Braaten and Roy A. Harrisville, *The Historical Jesus and Kerygmatic Christ* (New York: Abingdon, 1964). The monograph by James F. Peter, *Finding the Historical Jesus* (New York: Harper, 1965), is a careful account of the philosophical and theological background. Carl F. H. Henry edited an anthology specific to this problem that also includes essays on other questions of theology and history, *Jesus of Nazareth: Saviour and Lord* (Grand Rapids: Eerdmans, 1966). *Vindications: Essays on the Historical Basis of Christianity,* ed. Anthony Hanson (London: SCM, 1966), focuses on the question of the resurrection. It contains an especially compelling article by R. P. C. Hanson, "The Enterprise of Emancipating Christian Belief from History." And finally, since no bibliography on Christianity and history would be complete without citing the work of Wolfhart Pannenberg, we cite his *Jesus: God and Man* (Philadelphia: Westminster, 1968).

To conclude this introductory bibliography, we append several works that are useful to an understanding of the tradition of Christian views of history, particularly early Christian views. Roland Bainton and Erich Dinkler have chapters in *The Idea of History in the Ancient Near East* (New Haven: Yale, 1955) on patristic and earliest Christianity respectively. R. L. P. Milburn's Bampton Lectures of 1952, *Early Christian Interpretations of History* (New York: Harper, 1954), incorporate visual as well as verbal evidence. Lloyd G. Patterson, *God and History in Early Christian Thought* (New York: Seabury, 1967), studies the encounter between classical and Christian views down through Gregory the Great. And a concise and brilliant survey of the literary expression of Christian views of history is now to be found in C. A. Patrides, *The Grand Design of God: The Literary Form of the Christian View of History* (Toronto: University Press, 1972).

INDEX OF AUTHORS OF WORKS CITED
IN BIBLIOGRAPHY AND NOTES

INDEX OF MAJOR TOPICS AND THEMATIC GUIDE

Major themes that can be traced through several essays are indicated by asterisks (*). Other subjects are included if they are dealt with more than in passing.

(ABBREVIATIONS: B. = Herbert Butterfield; D. = Herman Dooyeweerd; L. = Kenneth Scott Latourette)